Battlegroun

ANZIO

Battleground series:

With the continued expansion of the Battleground Series a **Battleground Series Club** has been formed to benefit the reader. The purpose of the Club is to keep members informed of new titles and to offer many other reader-benefits. Membership is free and by registering an interest you can help us predict print runs and thus assist us in maintaining the quality and prices at their present levels.

Please call the office on 01226 734555, or send your name and address along with a request for more information to:

Battleground Series Club Pen & Sword Books Ltd,
47 Church Street, Barnsley, South Yorkshire S70 2AS

Overleaf: **Landing Ships Tank being loaded in the Bay of Naples for Anzio.**

Battleground Europe

ANZIO

IAN BLACKWELL

Pen & Sword
MILITARY

First published in Great Britain in 2006 by
Pen & Sword Military
an imprint of
Pen & Sword Books Ltd
47 Church Street
Barnsley
South Yorkshire
S70 2AS

ISBN 1 84415 473 4

A CIP catalogue record for this book is
available from the British Library.

Typeset in Palatino

Printed and bound in the United Kingdom by CPI

Pen & Sword Books Ltd incorporates the imprints of Pen & Sword Aviation, Pen
& Sword Maritime, Pen & Sword Military, Wharncliffe Local History, Pen and
Sword Select, Pen and Sword Military Classics and Leo Cooper.
For a complete list of Pen & Sword titles, please contact
Pen & Sword Books Limited
47 Church Street, Barnsley, South Yorkshire, S70 2AS, England
E-mail: enquiries@pen-and-sword.co.uk
Website: www.pen-and-sword.co.uk

CONTENTS

Ammunition being unloaded in Anzio harbour.

INTRODUCTION

The battle of Anzio lasted from 22 January to the 25 May 1944, when the Fifth Army linked up with the VI (US) Corps from the beachhead. Virtually all of the fighting took place in an area of about seven by fifteen miles, and involved thousands of men – and women – from several nations and belonging to a bewildering array of units, some of which saw the entire period through, others which came and went. Behind them, they left thousands of bodies.

In an area this small, inevitably, some ground was fought over time and again which makes it difficult to present a chronological account which neatly takes the reader – or even less so, the visitor – from point to point on the ground as the battle unfolded. As an example, the Via Anziate, the main road north from Anzio, was fought over for several weeks, while the struggle continued in other areas. To tell the story of the Via Anziate in isolation would present only a partial picture of what occurred during a period of time, and yet the story needs telling in the context of the ground, which was so important a factor in deciding the outcome of the fighting.

Historians of Anzio have approached it from several perspectives, ranging from the historical, political and strategic, to personal memoirs. The first level treats the subject almost as a chess game, seeing the actual participants as little more than pieces to be moved around the board, the second focuses in on small groups and individuals, most of whom are largely ignorant of the bigger picture – soldiers on the ground are like ants in a garden - they can see no further than the next pebble or blade of grass. It is here that the battle becomes very personal indeed, where the 'realities of war' are encountered. All of these standpoints are relevant and valid, and when put together contribute to a great body of information and analysis. A book of this length cannot hope to cover all of these, and yet some attempt must be made to address as many issues as possible, albeit in abbreviated form.

I have therefore elected to open this book with an overview of the battle from the strategic standpoint. This, I hope, sets the wider context as an aid to understanding why the battle was fought, before taking selected areas on the ground which are accessible today, which give some small flavour of the place in 1944, and, above all, which have a story to tell in terms of the conditions of warfare that the combatants experienced.

Any book of this length must necessarily be selective in the stories it tells, and I must therefore apologise to those readers who are hoping to find more information about particular events, units, or individuals. I hope that I have found examples which are representative of the times and of the conditions under which the battle was fought out.

A press release photograph at the time of the Anzio landings with the caption, 'Somewhere in Italy'.

ACKNOWLEDGEMENTS

One of the great pleasures in embarking on the research for this book has been in meeting so many extremely helpful people, for whom no request seems to have been too much trouble.

In particular I have to thank, in Italy, Alessandro Campagna and Roberto Molle of the Associazione Battaglia di Cassino, who have very kindly extended their interest from Cassino to join me in walking the ground at Anzio. Alessandro is responsible for recording veterans' accounts of the Italian campaign, and may be contacted at alessandrocampagna@libero.it – he would be delighted to hear from anyone who has a personal story. With the passing of the years the opportunity to collect these first-hand accounts diminishes, and this invaluable work should be encouraged wherever possible. Alessandro was kind enough to provide photographs and maps for this book, and to introduce me to Dottoressa Fiorenza Castaldi of the Comune di Pomezia who guided me around areas of the battlefield that I would otherwise not have had access to. I am indebted to Dottore Angelo Scimé for generously allowing her the time away from her desk to do this; and to Signore Bacoccoli who led me through the depths of the 'Boot' in February in pouring rain, which gave me a small inkling of what it must have been like there over sixty years ago.

In the United Kingdom I own a debt of gratitude to Chris Davis and Paul Hooton, whose interest in the Italian campaign has provided me with both practical support and much encouragement when working on this book. Also to the staff of the Prince Consort's Library, Aldershot, who have displayed remarkable patience in dealing with my innumerable requests for obscure volumes of military history, who have been extremely graceful in not pressing for the return of books when I have failed to send them back on time, and for their understanding when my aged dog took it into his head to devour one of their histories.

And to the officers and soldiers of those British Army regiments who have sought to develop their understanding of their profession through studying military history and visiting the battlefields, particularly those of the Italian campaign which have so many relevant lessons for coalition warfare.

Unless otherwise acknowledged, the photographs are courtesy of the Associazione Battaglia di Cassino.

ANZIO – AN OVERVIEW

ON 22 JANUARY 1944, four months after they invaded Italy, the Allies again made a seaborne landing on the Italian mainland. The operation was given the codename SHINGLE. Some thirty miles south of Rome and about seventy miles behind the German defences of the Gustav Line, a beachhead was established at Anzio by British and American troops of the VI (US) Corps. Anzio was to become one of the bloodiest battles fought by America and Britain during the Second World War, and one of the most controversial.

The town of Anzio is steeped in history. Known as Antium in Roman times, it was the birthplace of Nero, and it was here that he supposedly fiddled (or – more probably – played his lyre) while Rome burned. The insane emperor Caligula once proposed moving the capital to Antium from Rome, although it is unclear whether or not the idea was a product of his state of mind or based on more rational reasoning. In 445 AD the Vandals landed at the port before going on to sack Rome, and the Saracens destroyed the town some centuries later, after which the neighbouring town of Nettuno was established. As may be seen, the area had an unfortunate history, not helped by its location on the edge of the mosquito- and malaria-ridden Pontine Marshes which for centuries made it an unhealthy place to live. In 1928 Mussolini drained the marshes with a large ditch – named in his honour as the Mussolini Canal – into which ran a series of smaller canals to take the surface water into the sea. While this eased the problem of malaria, it presented another difficulty for soldiers, for the area south east of Anzio and Nettuno was, in effect, a network of anti-tank ditches. Before the war Anzio and Nettuno became popular seaside resorts, attracting numbers of holidaymakers from Rome.

Mussolini's engineers also constructed a number of show-piece modern Facist towns to accommodate farmworkers employed on the reclaimed land. One of these settlements north of Anzio, Aprilia, was to become known to the invaders as 'The Factory' because of the industrial appearance of the buildings. It consisted of some thirty buildings which included a church, town hall and the usual administrative offices of the local Facist Party and a military police barracks. On its southern edge was

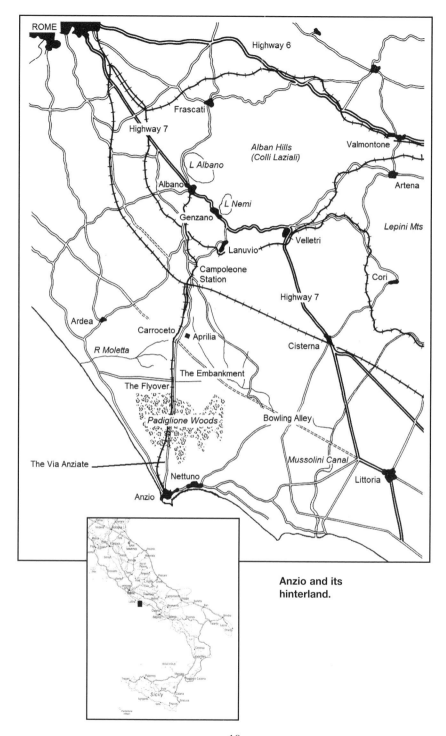

Anzio and its hinterland.

Carroceto, which in 1944 was little more than a railway station on the Rome-Anzio line. Both the town and the Mussolini Canal were to become better known for their part in the battles than for their enduring legacy to the foresight and planning of the Facist regime which built them for agricultural reasons.

The Roman road linking Anzio and Aprilia, the Via Anziate, runs on further northwards to Albano and the southern side of the Alban Hills, also known as the Colli Laziali. Here it joins Highway 7, the Appian Way, which is the southern road running from Rome to Naples, via Terracina on the coast. To the north of the Alban Hills runs Highway 6, the route from Rome to Naples via Valmontone and Frosinone, which follows the valley of the River Liri. About fifty miles east of Valmontone stands Monte Cassino and its monastery, which dominates the valley and the highway. The Alban Hills, which appear as a smudge on the horizon when seen from Anzio, assume a dominating height and commanding observation point when one stands upon them – it is difficult to conceal movement on the coastal plain from watchers on the hills. They are the last large geographical feature south of Rome and are the natural choice for a defensive line to protect the city.

Anzio before the war

American positions; the drainage problem is obvious, and soldiers began to experience trench foot and other complaints more familiar to the First World War than the Second.

On the plain to the east of the Via Anziate lies the network of canals and drainage ditches that were once the Pontine Marshes. To the west – south of Aprilia – is a deceptively flat area of ground that forms a plain stretching between the road and the River Moletta. The deception is that, on closer examination, this plain is scarred by gullies cut by the river and its tributaries, which are steep-sided and in places about fifty feet deep. To the British soldiers, bringing with them their years of experience and the language of North Africa, they were known as the Wadis. Despite the efforts of Mussolini's engineers the areas on the plain to both sides of the Via Anziate were poorly drained and the water table lay only a couple of feet below ground level, meaning that digging deeper than that resulted in a liquid-floored trench.

This, then, was the stage on which the battles of Anzio-Nettuno were fought in the first half of 1944, a stage which resembled an amphitheatre and on which a tragedy was to be played out.

The strategic situation

It goes almost without saying that all battles take place in the wider context of the war being fought, and of the political and strategic aims of the warring nations; but Anzio, perhaps more than most, was both the result of, and was affected by, the sometimes conflicting agendas of the British and American political and military leaders. The planning and execution of Operation SHINGLE were directly influenced by – on the one hand – the British wish to continue operations in the Mediterranean which had been underway since 1940, and – on the other – the American belief that the war against the Germans was best carried out by running down operations in the Mediterranean Theatre and diverting as many resources as possible, and at the earliest opportunity, to the United Kingdom in preparation for OVERLORD. The respective champions of these standpoints were Winston Churchill, the British Prime Minister, and General George C Marshall, the Chief of Staff of the American Army.

For the British, who had a long history of fighting a European foe elsewhere than in Europe itself (for example during the Seven Years' and Napoleonic Wars, where comparatively very little fighting took place against the French in France, but a considerable amount in the colonies or in allied countries such as Portugal) the opportunity to erode German strength through fighting them in the Mediterranean seemed a natural way to progress the war. Britain had a long association with the region, in particular with Gibraltar, Malta, Egypt and the route to India, and it was of great strategic interest to her; many campaigns had been fought there, with varying degrees of success – ranging from British naval and military victories during the Napoleonic Wars to the more ominous historical template, especially for Anzio, of the Gallipoli campaign of 1915-16.

For the Americans, the purpose was to get to grips with the enemy by the shortest way possible. France was directly en route from the United States to Berlin, and the idea that taking a detour to knock away Germany's Italian support would ultimately lead to Hitler's fall seemed less sensible than eliminating the Axis' strongest partner as a priority, after which everything else would be no more than a mopping-up operation. For the third major Allied power, Russia, the priority was to get the Americans and British to open the Second Front (by which they meant breaching the Atlantic Wall) to bring direct pressure on Germany and to provide support for the Red Army, which was then advancing in the east. The Russians had

Allied amphibious landings took place in North Africa, Sicily and on mainland Italy. Here a smoke screen covers the beach as troops disembark.

suffered casualty numbers far in excess of those of Britain and America, and Stalin was determined that his allies should play their full part in Hitler's downfall. To him also, the Mediterranean was a diversion which failed to meet his immediate objectives.

American forces had participated in the TORCH landings in North Africa in November 1942, but their performance at the Kasserine Pass had failed to impress both their more experienced British allies and their German enemies. Strategically and tactically, the Americans appeared naïve to the British. Their view of strategy seemed over-simplistic and lacking pragmatism; the commanders and troops on the ground were unpracticed and over-confident. This perception was to colour British attitudes for the future, despite the Americans' ability to learn and to fight in a much more professional manner in later engagements, for example in Sicily.

The wariness was not one-sided: for some Americans there was a suspicion that Churchill's obsession with the Mediterranean was a desire to avenge the Gallipoli fiasco. This mutual mistrust did not augur well for Allied operations.

The American presence in the Mediterranean was an indication of President Roosevelt's determination to come to grips with the Axis immediately after Pearl Harbor in December 1941, but the choice of theatre did not comply with the overall American concept of how the war should best be fought. The United States' strategic aim remained to follow the direct route to Germany, but, for the time being at any rate, this had to wait. Preparations for a landing in France would not be completed until May 1944, and the Western Allies could not remain inactive until then. Stalin was maintaining pressure to ensure that the Russians were not fighting the war on their own, but in any case it did not make sense to give the enemy a breathing space. For the short term, Americans would fight in the Mediterranean.

On 10 July 1943 TORCH was followed by HUSKY, the invasion of Sicily, and then by the invasion of mainland Italy across the Straits of Messina on 3 September that same year. These moves were a natural follow-on to the victory in North Africa, if only because of the proximity of Sicily and Italy. There was an air of inevitability to taking the war across these stepping stones into Europe, and was seen as a natural move by the British. However none of this, in American eyes, altered the status of north-west Europe rather than the Mediterranean as the primary route to finishing the war against Germany. There was a concern that Italy would swallow up troops which would be better employed elsewhere, and British thoughts of expanding operations elsewhere in the region, for example in the Aegean, were unwelcome. This antipathy was reflected in the allocation of resources, and the lack of a concerted Mediterranean strategy.

On 3 September the Allies crossed the Straits of Messina and began their progress up the toe of Italy. On 9 September the US Fifth Army, which comprised both American and British formations under General Mark Clark, landed at Salerno (Operation AVALANCHE). The British 1st Airborne Division landed at Taranto the same day, by sea. The Salerno landing had come as no real surprise to the Germans, who (like the Allied planners) had readily identified beaches close to a major port, Naples, which the Allies would need for a rapid build-up of forces, and which was within fighter cover of Sicilian airfields. Nor did the announcement of the Italian surrender, which had been negotiated secretly and which was made public by

Bren carriers coming ashore at Salerno. The close-run nature of the operation was to leave doubts in the minds of Generals Clark and Lucas about the feasibility of SHINGLE.

Eisenhower on the eve of AVALANCHE, influence events; the Germans, who distrusted their ally's commitment anyway, were ready to replace them in the defences. The landing was strongly opposed, so much so that at one stage General Clark considered evacuation of at least part of his forces. Montgomery's Eighth Army, meanwhile, was continuing to fight its own battles; no coordinated plan had been drawn up for the two formations to act in concert, and there was no immediate expectation that they would do so to resolve the Salerno problem. Its appearance after the crisis had passed, together with British press insinuations that Eighth Army had saved the day, only served to irritate Clark and to build upon the inter-Allied mistrust.

The overall strategy for Italy was poorly defined: there was no clearly agreed objective beyond creating a situation which would tie down as many German formations as possible and keep them from being redeployed to France. The purpose of invading Italy was to force an Italian surrender and to keep German troops from being used elsewhere. The first objective was achieved at an early date. Specifying Rome as the target was a belated decision, although Churchill had identified it as a desirable objective in May 1943, arguing that the city's capture would force the Germans back to the River Po, and that the fall of the first Axis capital would be a highly significant political and psychological move. It was only on 25 September that Eisenhower directed Alexander to take Rome. Even then, there was an uncertainty about the aims of the campaign in Italy. Its status as a sideshow to OVERLORD did not assist planners in producing a war-winning strategy for the Mediterranean theatre.

The Allied commanders began to put into practice the transfer of personnel and resources from the Mediterranean to the United Kingdom as the date for the cross-Channel invasion approached. Generals Eisenhower and Montgomery, Supreme Commander and Commander Eighth Army respectively, moved to England to prepare for OVERLORD. General Sir Henry Maitland Wilson became Supreme Commander Mediterranean, with Lieutenant General Jacob L Devers as his deputy and commander of the American forces in the Mediterranean. General Alexander was appointed Commander of the Allied Group of Armies in Italy (AAI). The British 7th Armoured, 50th (Northumberland) and 51st (Highland)

Divisions were withdrawn to England. American divisions which were moved from the Mediterranean included the 1st, 9th, and the 2nd Armored and most of 82nd Airborne. With them went their medical and logistic units. As if this depletion of the Allied forces in Italy were not enough, the proposed invasion of Southern France, for which planning was now underway, would place an additional demand upon the available resources, both human and materiel. The place of Italy in the grand scheme of things was to be little more than a diversion to draw as many German troops as possible away from the main targets. Regardless of this diminished role, those tasked with fighting in Italy were expected to be victorious.

The roads to Rome
The advance up the leg of Italy was a slow and laborious process. The width of the peninsula denied the Allies the possibility of outflanking the enemy except by sea. The hostile terrain – a backbone of mountains where the river valleys cut deeply across the line of advance – and the inventiveness and tenacity of the German defenders, together with the deteriorating weather, made progress a costly business. Faced with a resilient foe, the Allies turned again to the possibility of turning the defenders' lines by amphibious operations which became known as 'end runs' by the Americans, an expression derived from a tactic in American football whereby a player runs around the end of the gridlocked forwards rather than trying to batter a path through them. The term was less well understood by their allies, and Churchill had to have it explained to him in some detail. It was not the first, nor last, time that the Allies suffered from a degree of confusion about terminology; the problem was bad enough between the British and Americans, but it was compounded because in Italy there were representatives of many nations fighting on the same side, each with different cultures and using several languages: English, French, Italian, Arabic, Urdu, Polish, Greek, and Gurkhali to name but some of them. The Germans had a similar, although slightly less cosmopolitan problem, with soldiers from various European countries serving in their ranks; and they, too, had Italian troops under command from those units which had chosen to remain loyal to Mussolini and the Fascist cause after their country had surrendered.

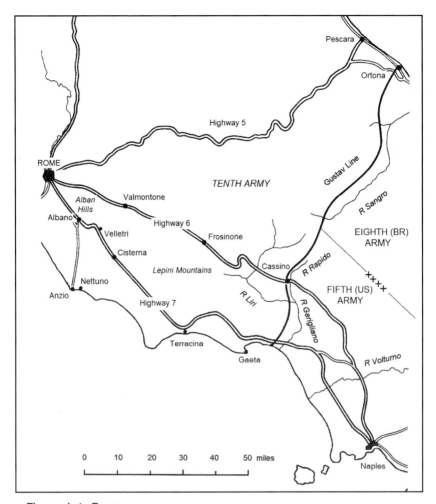

The roads to Rome.

The German defence of Italy was based upon a series of strongly held lines of resistance which stretched from the Adriatic to the Tyrrhenian Seas. From the toe of Italy northwards, the Allies encountered – one after the other – the Volturno, the Barbara, the Reinhard and lastly the Gustav Lines. The Allies had only limited options in dealing with the last of these because of the terrain and the deteriorating weather. The Eighth Army, advancing on the Adriatic coast, might have turned the Germans' flank from the north in fine weather, but

19

not in the mountain snows of winter. The most promising route to Rome was on the Fifth Army front, on the southern coast of Italy. But here the Gustav Line, running along the Garigliano River, was a formidable obstacle.

A seaborne landing on the Italian coast between the mouths of the Garigliano and the Tiber Rivers to outflank the German defences had been considered as early as November 1943. Plans were drawn up for a number of possible sites, including Anzio, but the evident strength of the Gustav Line indicated that a swift link-up between there and the beachhead was unlikely, and the plans were put aside for the time being. A major logistical limitation placed a constraint on amphibious operations: two-thirds of the ninety Landing Ships Tank (LSTs) in the Mediterranean were to sail to Britain by 15 December 1943, in preparation for the cross-Channel invasion. Before that date, they were fully employed in transporting troops and materiel from Sicily and North Africa to Italy, to build up as many forces there as possible before their withdrawal, and there was little flexibility as to when they would be available to mount a landing.

Notwithstanding this problem, the senior Allied commanders in the Mediterranean were in agreement that, if at all possible, a landing should be made to support the advance

Landing Ships Tank (LSTs), upon which Operation SHINGLE depended

on Rome. General Alexander gave orders to Fifth Army to develop a plan to put a force ashore south of Rome to capture the Alban Hills, which were the last defensible position before the city. On 25 November, General Clark approved the plan for a landing to take place at Anzio once the Fifth Army had got near Frosinoni, about forty miles southeast of Rome. The Anzio force was to be a comparatively small one and its purpose was only to assist Fifth Army in capturing the Alban Hills; the two bodies of troops were to link up no more than seven days after the landing. Clark's plan effectively reversed the roles of the two forces; whereas Alexander intended the Anzio troops to take the Alban Hills, Clark had Fifth Army doing this. At the time, the difference seemed immaterial, because it appeared that the operation would be delayed indefinitely because the combination of enemy resistance, bad weather and mountainous country was slowing the Fifth Army advance so much that it could not get to the Frosinoni area to carry out its part in the plan.

On 10 December the project was revived when General Clark suggested that a landing, by a larger force than that previously contemplated and given adequate seaborne support to keep it resupplied, would present the Germans with a threat which they could not ignore, even if the force were to remain static rather than moving on Rome. Having to deal with it would draw German forces away from the Gustav Line and make Fifth Army's advance easier. Eight days later the idea was dropped because it was felt that there was not enough time to put together the plan before the cut-off date of 15 January.

At Tunis Churchill refused to abandon the issue, and he put pressure on the British Chiefs of Staff to use the plan for the Anzio landing to break the Italian stalemate. On Christmas Day 1943, both Churchill and Alexander argued forcefully for the idea. No longer was there a suggestion that there be a strictly limited period for the landing force to hold on to the beachhead before Fifth Army linked up with it; the possibility of supplying it by sea, together with the perceived strategic value of placing a threat behind German lines, proved highly attractive, at least to the British who were wedded to a Mediterranean strategy.

For the operation to succeed, however, it was essential that sufficient LSTs be made available. Churchill appealed directly to Roosevelt for fifty-six of these vessels to be kept in Italy until 5

February. Roosevelt acquiesced, but set the date as 3 February. The on-off nature of the operation, to be carried out in the depths of winter with such time constraints, did not promise well for its smooth execution.

The Allied planners drew up revised plans for the landing, based upon the earlier ideas. It would be made by VI (US) Corps comprising two divisions with armoured forces and supported by paratroops; the total troop numbers would be more than twice those in the original plan. The landing was to be between 20 and 31 January 1944, with the preference for as early a date as possible, to allow flexibility in the event of bad weather. Once again, this operation was to coincide with those on the Gustav Line, where the intention was for Fifth Army, supported by two divisions from the Eighth Army, to break through the German defences and then push up the Liri Valley towards Rome. This attack would be in sufficient strength to draw in the enemy reserves, at which point the amphibious landing would be made at Anzio-Nettuno. The area selected for the landing measured some fifteen miles wide by seven deep, bounded by the Molatta River to the northwest and the Mussolini Canal to the southeast. These features gave a natural defensive line behind which the Allies could establish a firm base. The seaborne troops would then advance inland towards the Alban Hills, capture of which would block the German lines of communication between Rome and the Gustav Line.

The planners believed that the Germans lacked the strength to deal with threats to both their front and rear, and that they would have to withdraw units from the Gustav Line to counter the attack. Fifth and Eighth Armies were to take advantage of this to drive forward towards Rome, Fifth to link up with the Anzio force via Highway 6 in the Liri Valley, and Eighth to cut Highway 5 via Pescara.

A Fifth Army intelligence summary for 16 January deduced that German strength facing them on the Gustav Line was declining, because of 'casualties, exhaustion, and possibly lowering of morale.' There were no fresh German reserves, and very few tired ones – their entire strength would be required to defend the current positions. A coordinated Allied attack on the German line through Cassino would be unlikely to be resisted strongly: 'Since this attack is to be launched before SHINGLE, it is considered likely that this additional threat will cause him to withdraw from his defensive position once he has appreciated the magnitude of that operation.'

Allied intelligence believed the German reserves to be one division and four parachute battalions, with an additional armoured and an antitank battalion and miscellaneous minor units. Altogether these totaled about 14,300 men in the Rome area, and would be available to the Germans on the first day of the Allied landings. On the following day, D+1, a further division, an *SS* infantry regiment, a combat team from *XIV Panzer Corps*, and possibly elements of the *Hermann Göring Panzer Division* could be assembled to counter the landing. By D+2 at the earliest, it was felt that the Germans would have realized that Eighth Army had been depleted to provide some of the troops at Anzio, and could release *26th Panzer Division* from the front facing them. This would bring German strength opposing VI (US) Corps to 31,000 men. By D+16 the German strength was forecast to be 61,300, which would considerably outnumber the Allied troops in the beachhead. The lesson to be drawn from these calculations was that Allied action had to be swift if SHINGLE's objectives were to be attained.

So much for Allied expectations of what the Germans could do. It is appropriate here to consider the enemy's preparations for dealing with the eventuality of a landing in their rear. German intelligence about a forthcoming landing was

Postcards of Anzio were sold to Allied soldiers in Naples before the invasion; but no-one told the Germans

Anzio. La Spiaggia di Levante.

negligible. Although Kesselring's staff clearly recognized that an 'end run' was on the cards, and had identified four potential sites where such an operation might take place, the specific location and date for SHINGLE had not been discovered. Despite the accumulation of shipping in Naples, and the eagerness of local touts to sell postcards of Anzio to anyone interested, word had not got back to German headquarters about the forthcoming operation. The *Luftwaffe* had failed to spot anything which hinted at preparations for a landing; the sky was not as free to them as it once had been, and reconnaissance missions were becoming increasingly difficult.

Vague expectations of an Allied landing had been voiced in the German headquarters. German coastal troops had been on a heightened state of alert for some days in anticipation of a landing – possibly to take place at Civitavecchia – but they could not maintain this level for too long, and on the night of 22 January they stood down, relatively confident that there was no immediate danger. Kesselring was also reassured by the visit of

Admiral Canaris, the head of German military intelligence, the *Abwehr*, who stated that there was no sign that a landing would occur in the near future. Canaris left Kesselring's headquarters on 21 January – the day before SHINGLE. There was a major failing of intelligence, and the Germans were given no warning of it at all.

Kesselring had, however, prepared contingency plans to deal with landings at several points along the coast. That dealing with one in the Rome area was codenamed *CASE RICHARD*. It identified reserves that could be assembled at short notice, mostly from the *Fourteenth Army* on coast-watching duties or undergoing training in northern Italy, but also from southern France and in the Balkans. The routes which these units would take to get to the landing area

Generalfeldmarschall Albert Kesselring

24

had been carefully identified and stockpiles of fuel established to ensure that there would be no delay in bringing them forward. Close to river crossing sites engineers had pontoon equipment prepared, to replace bridges that might have been destroyed by Allied bombing as part of the preparation for isolating the beachhead. In immediate reserve, to seal any landing area until more substantial forces could be gathered, Kesselring had taken two divisions from the *Tenth Army* and positioned them near Rome.

The Fifth Army attacks which were launched on the Garigliano and Rapido Rivers during January put more pressure on the Germans than the Allies realized at the time. X (British) Corps mounted attacks on the Gustav Line on 17 January, which General Clark intended to support an offensive made by II (US) Corps to enter the Liri Valley. On 20 January 36th (US) Division launched its ill-fated attempt to cross the Rapido. The details of these operations do not concern us here, except in that they affected the disposition of German forces in Italy. With his right wing being threatened, and with only second-rate troops to deal with the Allied offensive, General von Vietinghoff requested reinforcements for his *Tenth Army*.

With a degree of confidence that no landing was imminent, Kesselring authorized the dispatch south of the major parts of *29th* and *90th Panzer Grenadier Divisions* and part of the *Hermann Göring Panzer Division*. Believing that there was no immediate threat to Rome and that the Allied thrust was concentrated on the Gustav Line, Kesselring reasoned that the two divisions would stabilize the situation there. They could then return to Rome if circumstances so demanded.

The dates and the locations selected for the landings presented the Allied planners with difficulties – given the speed with which the operation was mounted, during the winter months, it could hardly be otherwise. The possibility of bad weather – rain and low clouds which would reduce visibility and hinder air operations, and high seas – was to be expected in January, and an average of only two good days was to be expected each week. The beaches chosen for the landings were shallower than those at Salerno, and there were two sandbanks offshore which would restrict the types of vessels able to be employed; only the smaller landing craft (LCVP – Landing Craft, Vehicles and Personnel; LCA – Landing Craft, Assault;

and DUKWs – 2½-ton amphibious trucks) were expected to be suitable outside the immediate area of Anzio harbour itself. It was hoped that the port would be captured intact before the Germans had time to destroy its facilities; without its use, the landing force would face a much more difficult logistic problem.

Air preparation for the landings was to be provided by the Allied Tactical and Strategic Air Forces, which would bomb enemy airfields and attempt to cut the routes to the beachhead. After the Allies were ashore, the Air Forces were to try to isolate the beachhead by refusing the Germans access. The raw statistics illustrate their confidence in their ability to do just this. Altogether some 2,600 Allied aircraft were available in Italy, Corsica and Sardinia, which represented an overwhelming superiority over the *Luftwaffe* forces in the Mediterranean theatre. German aircraft, not including transport and coastal, numbered 242 at the end of December 1943, of which only 121 were serviceable; a further eighty-two were based in southern France. In the lead-up to the landings, 5,777 tons of bombs were dropped and 12,974 sorties flown against the *Luftwaffe* and rail communications in Italy; during the week immediately preceding D-Day 6,471 tons were dropped and 9,876 sorties flown against roads and railways north of Rome and those leading to Anzio. On 22 January itself the Allies flew 1,200 sorties compared to 140 by the *Luftwaffe*. There was no question as to which side dominated the skies over Italy. Nevertheless, when the time came the *Luftwaffe* was able to inflict damage on the invaders.

The final plans for the landings were agreed on 12 January. The problems over shipping had been largely resolved by Churchill and Roosevelt, and troops had been allocated to tasks. At the beginning of the operation VI (US) Corps would be made up of the following formations and units, which totalled about four divisions:

3rd (US) Division, under Major General Lucian K Truscott, comprising 7, 15 and 30 Infantry Regiments.

504 Parachute Infantry Regiment.

509th Parachute Infantry Battalion.

1st, 3rd and 4th Ranger Infantry Battalions.

751st Tank Battalion.

1st (US) Armored Division, under Major-General E. N. Harmon, comprising 1 Armored Regiment and 6 Armored

Infantry Regiment.

1st (British) Infantry Division, under Major-General W. R. C. Penney, comprising 2 and 3 Infantry and 24 Guards Brigades, and 46th Royal Tank Regiment.

2 Special Service Brigade, comprising the 9th and 43rd (Royal Marine) Commandos.

The plan for the landing itself identified three beaches on which the Allies would descend upon the area around Anzio and Nettuno:

3rd (US) Division would land on X RAY Red and Green Beaches, to the south of Anzio and Nettuno, followed by 504 Parachute Infantry Regiment.

1st, 3rd and 4th Ranger Infantry Battalions would land on X RAY Yellow Beach and take the port of Anzio, followed by the 509th Parachute Infantry Battalion.

The British 2 Brigade Group, consisting of 2 Brigade and 1st Battalion The Scots Guards (from 24 Guards Brigade, under command for the landing), and followed by 2 Special Service Brigade, would land on PETER Beach six miles to the north-east of Anzio.

As a floating reserve, the remainder of 1st (British) Division, with 46th Royal Tank Regiment, 24 Field and 50 Medium Regiments Royal Artillery, would remain afloat until called forward. 504 Parachute Infantry Regiment would land behind 3rd (US) Division, also as Corps reserve.

In command of VI Corps was Major General John P Lucas. His background included commanding 3rd (US) Division when it had trained in the United States before embarking for overseas duty, and he had been Eisenhower's 'personal representative' on the ground during the Sicilian campaign, at the end of which he replaced Bradley as the commander of II (US) Corps. Eleven days after the Salerno landing, he assumed command of VI Corps, replacing the general whose performance during that particular operation had been found wanting. In mid-January Lucas reached his fifty-

Major General John P Lucas.

fourth birthday, but he appeared to many to be – and he himself felt – somewhat older. The months of mountain fighting which his corps had undertaken had taken a toll on him.

Late in December 1943 Lucas was informed that VI Corps was to carry out the Anzio landing. He had little optimism about the prospects for success, noting in his diary, 'these 'Battles of the Little Big Horn' aren't much fun and a failure now would ruin Clark, probably kill me, and certainly prolong the war.' After attending a conference at which Alexander stated that the operation would proceed on 22 January, with no more troops than had been already assigned, he wrote, 'I felt like a lamb being led to the slaughter... the whole affair has a strong odor of Gallipoli and apparently the same amateur was still on the coach's bench.'

A major contributory factor to the later debate about the success or otherwise of the operation is the interpretation of the various commanders' expectations and the clarity – or otherwise – of the orders they issued. The more optimistic of the Allied commanders took the view that the Anzio operation would draw German reserves away from the Gustav Line, and that a breakthrough could be swiftly achieved, which would permit an early link-up with the Anzio force. Furthermore, capturing Rome, the first of the enemy capitals, would be a major coup which would signal the inevitability of an Allied victory: a highly significant political and psychological stroke. Churchill's hope was that 'we were hurling a wild cat on the shore', a somewhat more energetic concept than actually transpired. Admiral Sir John Cunningham was only marginally less forceful in talking of a 'lightning thrust by two or three divisions'. The Operation Instruction from Alexander's Headquarters dated 12 January 1944 explained that 'the objects of this operation will be to cut the enemy's main communications in the Colli Laziali area south-east of Rome, and to threaten the rear of the German 14 Corps'. Further yet down the chain of command came Clark's Field Order, which gave the aims as '(a) To seize and secure a beachhead in the vicinity of Anzio; (b) Advance on Colli Laziali.' Lucas' own VI Corps Field Order stated that his formation would seize and secure the beachhead and advance in the direction of Colli Laziali. The aggressiveness of the operation became steadily more diluted the lower down the chain of command – and the

Generals Clark and Alexander. Each had a different perception of the aim of SHINGLE, and they were to differ again when the question of capturing Rome arose later in the year. Presenting of the ribbon of Knight Commander of the British Empire 29 April 1944.

closer it came to having to actually put the concept into practice – one went.

At the back of the minds of both Clark and Lucas was the Salerno landing, only four months earlier. A repeat of such a close-run thing was not to be countenanced. And Lucas was not alone among senior officers who had studied the Great War and the failed Gallipoli expedition, and who saw uncomfortable parallels, particularly with the Suvla landings. There, in an attempt to break the deadlock at Helles, where British, ANZAC and French troops could not progress against the Turkish defences, a landing had been made further up the Gallipoli peninsula. As was to occur at Anzio, the force commander chose to establish a firm beachhead before pushing inland, an action which allowed the Turks to seal off the landing area before the British could achieve their objectives. If Lucas had taken the lessons of Suvla to heart, he might have been more aggressive; but he might also be remembered for throwing away VI Corps on an unsupported and futile expedition deep into enemy-held territory.

Preparations for SHINGLE
Preliminary reconnaissance of the beaches had been carried out by Combined Operations Pilotage Parties, teams recruited mainly from the Royal Navy and Royal Engineers, and by members of the Special Boat Section They were launched in two-man collapsible canvas canoes known as folboats from submarines or small boats at night, and paddled close to shore where one of the team would swim ashore to investigate the defences and technical details such as the gradient and geological composition of the beach. He had then to return to the canoe, which in turn had to find the submarine in the darkness. It is believed that at least two of these teams were lost

3rd Ranger Battalion embarking in Naples.

LSTs loading in Naples.

off Anzio, which seems a surprisingly low casualty rate given the inherent dangers of the mission.

Rehearsal time for SHINGLE was short. Despite General Lucas' request for a delay to permit him to ready his corps for the landing, no leeway was given to him, and practice only commenced in early January, in the Naples area. The programme culminated in a Corps exercise, WEBFOOT, which ran from 17 to 19 January. This was a practice landing south of Salerno, but it was far from being a success – or for raising Lucas' confidence. The British experience during the exercise was relatively successful, but 3rd (US) Division lost forty DUKWs and nineteen 105-mm howitzers – a battalion of field artillery – sunk when the DUKWs foundered having been launched too far offshore in bad weather. Although loss of life was not heavy, the battalion had to be replaced by one from 45th

(US) Division before SHINGLE. Not a single American unit was landed in the right place, or at the right time. This was only five days before the actual invasion.

The Allied deception plan was designed to convince the Germans that a landing, when it came, would be north of Rome. Troops and landing craft were brought to Sardinia and Corsica, and heavy bombing raids were carried out against Civitavecchia and locations in northern Italy. Fake wireless messages were sent reinforcing this illusory plan, but in codes known to be able to be read by the Germans. Despite the short preparation time, the deception proved extremely successful.

To achieve surprise on the day of the landings itself, there was to be no prolonged naval bombardment of the selected beaches; instead, three Landing Crafts Tank (Rocket) [LCT(R)s] were to deliver their rockets between H-10 and H-5 minutes. To provide a diversion from the Anzio area, a small naval task force was to shell the port of Civitavecchia, on the coastline north of Rome at the time that the Anzio landing was launched. This, together with the deception plan which had hinted heavily that Civitavecchia was to be the target, was to be sufficient to cause Kesselring to order its immediate destruction to prevent it falling into Allied hands.

The Landings

The invasion fleet, Task Force 81, set sail from Naples, Salerno, and lesser ports in the Bay of Naples during the late afternoon and evening of 20 January. To screen its objective from German agents, it sailed southwards around the Isle of Capri before altering course towards its destination. Shortly after midnight on the night of 21-22 January it arrived off Anzio, where the groups of ships assigned to particular beaches were guided to their locations by beacon submarines, HMS *Ultor* and *Uproar*, before they dropped anchor.

The troops climbed into their assault craft which then formed up into their formations for the landing and moved towards the beaches. At 0150 hours, ten minutes before H Hour, the LCT(R)s launched their missiles – 785 five-inch rockets – at selected targets ashore. There was no return fire, to the surprise and delight of many of those in the Allied force, and the first wave of assault craft hit the beaches at 0200 hours as planned.

On the British beach west of Anzio, PETER, the leading

A Bren carrier landing.

Peter Beach.

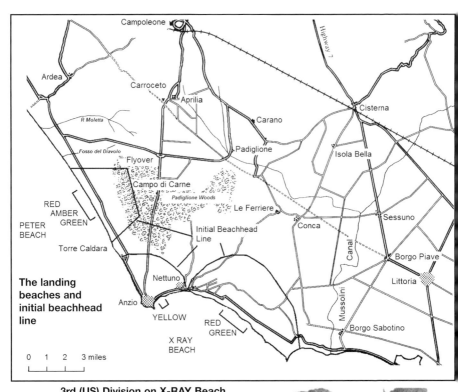

The landing beaches and initial beachhead line

0 1 2 3 miles

3rd (US) Division on X-RAY Beach.

By the end of D-Day, the Allies had landed some 36,000 men.

troops of 2 (British) Infantry Brigade Group faced an offshore sandbank, which prevented some landing craft from reaching the beach, and poor exit routes inland once the beach had been reached. The first wave was all ashore by 0245 hours, followed by 2 Special Service Brigade. The remainder of 24 Guards Brigade was landed by 1130 hours.

2 Brigade advanced through the scrubland as the day progressed, and by nightfall the Loyals were firm on the Fosso del Diavolo, with the North Staffordshires on the west end of the Campo di Carno ridge. The Gordons were to their right rear. 2 Special Service Brigade was two and a half miles north of Anzio on the Via Anziate; and 24 Guards Brigade was near Torre Caldara.

In the port of Anzio (X RAY Yellow Beach) the Ranger Battalions landed followed by 509th Parachute Infantry Battalion. The Rangers' assault vessels were guided to their destination by a US Navy ensign in a folboat, who signalled the way with a yellow lamp. The only enemy unit in the town, an engineer battalion from *29th Panzer Grenadier Division*, which had been sent to Anzio to rest and to practice a little demolition by blowing up the harbour, was taken by surprise and many of its personnel were captured whilst still abed. Once the Rangers had taken Anzio, the paratroopers of 509th Parachute Infantry Battalion, followed by 504 Parachute Infantry Regiment, advanced eastwards and took Nettuno. The harbour of Anzio was captured without any significant damage having been done to it, and it was cleared for use by Allied shipping by early afternoon.

On X-RAY Red and Green Beaches, east of Nettuno, 3rd (US) Division established itself ashore, encountering only scattered enemy patrols. 30 Regiment pushed inland towards Le Ferriere and Conca and had captured the main bridges over the western branch of the Mussolini Canal by sundown.

By the end of D-Day, the Allies had landed some 36,000 men and more than 3,000 vehicles, together with several tons of supplies – about ninety per cent of the embarked force. Casualties had been remarkably light: thirteen dead, ninety-seven wounded and forty-four missing. 227 prisoners were taken. So far, so good.

The German reaction

The first reports of the landing were delivered by a German railway engineer corporal, who rode his motorcycle to Albano in an attempt to make his report. He met a German *Panzer Grenadier* lieutenant who was passing through, who in his turn informed the Town Major, who sent the news to Rome, where it was received at about 0400 hours. Kesselring was swift to react. He quickly grasped the seriousness of the situation and ordered *CASE RICHARD* to be implemented. Units were summoned from Italy, Germany, France and Yugoslavia to respond to the threat.

Kesselring's immediate aim was to seal off the beachhead. Three divisions in reserve in northern Italy, under command of *Fourteenth Army*, were on the move south within twenty-four hours, but there were more immediately available units closer to Anzio, and these were assembled to form a ring around the landing area. The counterattack that the Germans were preparing on the Garigliano River front was cancelled, and units freed to move to Anzio. This decision was a calculated risk, for Kesselring interpreted the landing as an Allied move to weaken his defences on the Gustav Line – in fact, the original objective of SHINGLE before it had gone through its metamorphosis and become an attempt to seize the Alban Hills... depending upon the views of the particular Allied commander.

Ready to hand in the Anzio area the Germans had less than

1,000 men, but more were available at short notice. Three battalions of *90th Panzer Grenadier Division* were north of Rome and *Battle Group Gericke* of the *4th Parachute Division* was further inland. The main elements of this division were at Spoleto, north of Rome. Near Velletri were two parachute engineer companies from the same division, and a battle group from *29th Panzer Grenadier Division*. A reconnaissance battalion was near Terracina, and in the Alban Hills were reinforcement holding units of the *Hermann Göring Division*. The *71st Infantry* and the *3rd Panzer Grenadier Divisions* were to the south, moving towards the Gustav Line, and were recalled, and the first units from them began to arrive on 23 January. The *Luftwaffe* anti-aircraft commander in the Rome area rapidly moved his guns to positions circling the exits from the beachhead.

To command and control this motley group of units, Kesselring first appointed Brigadier General Schlemmer, a staff officer and former commandant of Rome. His failure to follow Kesselring's orders to seal the beachhead – he started to group infantry battalions in the Alban Hills as a reserve, rather than using them to block key points – led to his swift replacement by General Schlemm, commander of *I Parachute Corps*. While their names may have appeared similar, their performance was not.

General Eberhard von Mackensen. He was put in command of the defences at Anzio.

Schlemm both understood what he should be doing and was capable of doing it.

On 24 January Kesselring ordered the *Fourteenth Army*, under General Eberhard von Mackensen, to take control of the Anzio defences. When he assumed command the following day, von Mackensen had elements of eight divisions deployed around the beachhead, with five more divisions and supporting units on the way. He divided the perimeter into sectors, and by 28 January the eastern defences in front of Cisterna were under command of the *Hermann Göring Panzer Division*, the centre under *3rd Panzer Grenadier Division*, and the western – behind the Moletta River – under *65th Infantry*

Division. Making use of *Fourteenth Army* to fight the Anzio battle left *Tenth Army* to concentrate on the Gustav Line, a sensible and practical course of action which ensured that each army focused on its own personal war. Kesselring, of course, maintained a lofty overview of proceedings on both fronts, and was in turn overseen from Berlin.

The Germans were not only helped by their contingency planning and the availability of troops to form the cordon. Luck played its part when a copy of the SHINGLE plan fell into German hands on the first day, carried by an Allied officer who was taken prisoner. The Germans had a full briefing on their enemy's intentions.

Expanding the beachhead
Many of the troops who landed on 22 January wondered what they should have been doing – they were certainly not pushing forcefully inland, and with no sign of German resistance they wondered why not. But General Lucas was more concerned

Early days – the illusion of success.

with establishing his base than thrusting towards Rome, or even towards the Alban Hills. Lucas had qualms about risking his force unnecessarily, and he was reinforced in these worries by a visit by Generals Alexander and Clark during the afternoon of D-Day, when Clark took him aside and advised him 'Don't stick your neck out Johnny. I did at Salerno and got into trouble.' Lucas felt confident that he was doing the right thing, and indeed had reason to feel satisfied with what had been achieved during the day. What may have appeared right to Lucas and Clark, however, would not have seemed right to Churchill, had he known that VI Corps was not about to move onto the Alban Hills. For his part, Alexander expressed satisfaction to Lucas about the progress of the landings and appeared to realise that the corps was not sufficiently strong at this stage to make the attempt to move deep inland.

Lucas knew that as a minimum he had to seize Albano and Campoleone. Control of these two towns would block German road and rail movement southwards – but only on Highway 7. Unless he could also cut Highway 6, to the north of the Alban Hills, the enemy still had a viable route, the more important one, between Rome and the Gustav Line. With only two divisions, he could not hope to block both highways, let alone maintain a secure link with the beachhead. If its objective was to capture the hills, the SHINGLE plan was seriously flawed.

However happy Lucas may have been that he was doing the correct thing for the moment, he was storing up trouble for the future. The longer he waited before advancing, the more opportunity Kesselring had to assemble his forces to counter him. The fact that the Allies had failed to break through the Gustav Line, and did not appear able to do so in the immediate future, meant that the Germans felt free to withdraw units from there to deal with SHINGLE, should the need arise. Additionally, of course, there would be time to bring up the formations as planned for in *CASE RICHARD*.

The build-up of VI Corps and expansion of the beachhead.
On D+1, 23 January, the remainder of 1st (British) Division landed at Anzio, and the following day 179 Regimental Combat Team (RCT – roughly equivalent to a British brigade) of the 45th (US) Division arrived. The rest of the division and the 1st (US) Armored Division (less Combat Command B) were also called

American troops on the Mussolini Canal, which formed the eastern beachhead defence line. Note that the GI kneeling on the left has picked up a German sniper's K98k carbine.

forward to the beachhead. Two days later, 2 Special Service Brigade, their part in the initial landing done, returned to the Garigliano. On January 25, PETER Beach was closed and Anzio port and X RAY Yellow Beach were used instead.

On January 24, 1st (British) Division closed up to the Moletta River. A patrol of the 5th Grenadier Guards, sent to reconnoitre towards Albano, found Aprilia held by troops of the *3rd Panzer Grenadier Division*. The next day, the Guards, supported by a squadron of Sherman tanks of the 46th RTR, captured the town and with it 111 prisoners.

To anyone hoping for a dash to seize Rome, progress inland was painfully slow. On January 26, the Grenadier and Irish Guards repulsed a German counter-attack which yielded another forty-six prisoners. Enemy resistance was beginning to shape up, and VI Corps could no longer hope for a smooth passage.

To the east, the Americans were less successful in their dealings with the enemy. On 24 January, patrols pushed towards Cisterna, in the face of German resistance. The following day two American battalions advanced on the town: the first moved only a mile and a half up the Conca road before being halted; the other was stopped by a company from the *Hermann Göring Panzer Division* at a road junction some two miles past the western branch of the Mussolini Canal.

Further attempts on 26 and 27 January moved 3rd (US) Division no closer than three miles to Cisterna. 504 Parachute Infantry Regiment made a diversionary attack to the east across the main Mussolini Canal, and captured the villages of Sessano, Borgo Piave and Borgo Sabatini, before being driven out by a counterattack, again by elements of the *Hermann Göring Panzer Division*. The situation on the beachhead was becoming less promising by the moment.

By 28 January VI Corps had landed about 69,000 men, 237 tanks and 508 artillery pieces of various calibres, as well as 27,250 tons of supplies. But by now, a week after the landing, the Germans had an equivalent-size force surrounding the beachhead. Despite Allied air superiority, German bombing raids and artillery bombardments were increasing, and no area was out of their range. From the evening of 22 January onwards, German aircraft had made attacks on Allied shipping despite taking losses. On 23 January the destroyer HMS *Janus* was sunk and HMS *Jervis* damaged. Allied reaction was to withdraw the cruisers HMS *Penelope*, *Orion* and *Spartan* out of danger from air attack, their firepower not being required by the land forces. The following day there were two more attacks at dusk, by forty-three and fifty-two bombers respectively. For a loss of eleven aircraft, the Germans succeeded in sinking the hospital ship *St David* and damaging her sister ship *Leinster*, the destroyer USS *Plunkett* and a minesweeper, the USS *Prevail*. The USS *Mayo* was damaged by a mine. The honeymoon period that had begun so promisingly on the morning of 22 January was definitely short-lived.

Germans renewed their air attacks on the evening of 26 January. They lost nine bombers, but sank HMS *Spartan*, which had returned from Naples, and the cargo ship *Samuel Huntington* on 29 January, with heavy loss of life. By this time, on land, 24 Guards Brigade had pushed forward some one and a half miles north of the Factory area.

The Allied advance out of the beachhead.
Generals Alexander and Clark visited the beachhead again on 25 January, and two days later Alexander pressed for an advance towards Velletri on Highway 7. On 28 January Clark returned to Anzio, a trip which was not without its drama, for his PT boat was mistaken for an E-Boat and fired on by an

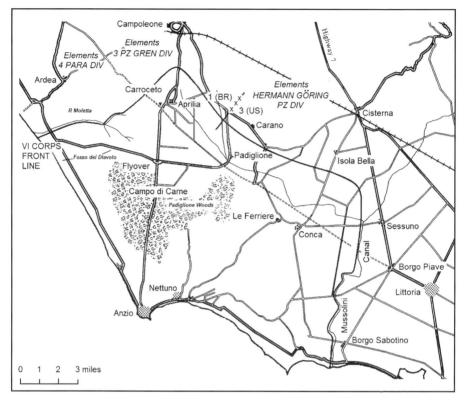

VI Corps Front Line on 28 January.

American minesweeper, causing casualties amongst the crew, although Clark himself escaped unscathed. Clark urged Lucas to capture Cisterna and Campoleone, which would give him control of the two road centres from which he could move onto the Alban Hills. The road centres may have been key points for the Allies, but the geography of the area dictated that they would be of universal military interest. These towns also controlled the German routes for attacks on the beachhead, and featured prominently in General von Mackensen's plans to eradicate it. By 30 January he had assembled four large battle groups under command of *I Parachute Corps*, totalling thirty-three battalions, to put his plan into effect. The stage was set for a collision between two armies both set on attacking.

The VI Corps' plan was for a two-pronged attack on the Alban Hills, and was based on the assumption that the Germans held Cisterna and Campoleone only as screening or delaying positions in front of their main defence line further north in the Hills. Contradicting this assessment, 1st (British) Division's intelligence staff had identified the German main line of resistance as passing through these towns, and also that the enemy was preparing a counterattack. On the German side, *Fourteenth Army* staff believed that the Allies had landed three infantry and one armoured divisions, which would be insufficient for an attack on the Alban Hills because there would not be enough troops to protect the flanks of such an advance. In the expectation that the Allies needed more time to establish the beachhead and build up their strength for a later date, von Mackensen planned to strike first.

To the east, Lucas' plan was that 3rd (US) Division, with 504 Parachute Infantry Regiment and the three Ranger battalions, would cut Highway 7 at Cisterna before advancing on Valmontone and Highway 6. To the west, the main thrust was to be made by 1st (British) Division up the Via Anziate towards Albano and Genzano. To the left of the British advance, Combat Command A of 1st (US) Armored Division was to hook north-west with the objective of taking Campoleone from the west. This plan made it necessary to reorganise troops on the ground before it could be put into practice, freeing some from defensive tasks to allow their participation in the attacks, and 36 (US) Engineer Regiment therefore relieved 2 (British) Infantry Brigade on the Fosso della Moletta; 1st Reconnaisance Regiment relieved the Rangers and 3rd Battalion of 7 (US) Infantry Regiment east of Aprilia; and part of 179 (US) RCT relieved 504 Parachute Infantry Regiment on the Mussolini Canal. These preparations, a complicated-sounding reshuffling of bodies of men around the battlefield, further delayed the attack, which unbeknownst to the Allies allowed the Germans more time to assemble their own forces for the attack that they themselves were planning.

The American attack
On the eastern flank General Truscott envisaged three axes of advance towards Cisterna. Two Ranger battalions were to infiltrate the town before dawn, to divert attention from the main attack. The third Ranger battalion and a battalion from 15 Infantry Regiment were to advance up the Conca-Cisterna road

itself, via Isola Bella; and a mile to the west, 7 Infantry Regiment would advance northwards to capture the railway line west of Cisterna, and then Highway 7 north of the town. To cover the right flank of these advances 504 Parachute Infantry was make a diversionary attack northwards along the Mussolini Canal. This operation is described in detail in Chapter 4, and the story will not be repeated here, other than to record that it was a disaster for the American forces, which lost two Ranger battalions and other forces when they ran into German formations that von Mackensen was concentrating in the area for his planned counterattack on the beachhead.

The Americans had pushed their line only about one and a half miles forward. General Truscott decided to renew his attack on the following day, 31 January, using all of his artillery and with tanks and tank destroyers in support. He also brought up the 1st Battalion of 30 Infantry Regiment from reserve. From the area of Ponte Rocco 7 Infantry, and from Isola Bella 15 Infantry Regiments were to converge upon Cisterna. Until noon on 1 February, the battle swung back and forth as Americans attacked and Germans counterattacked, by which time the line had been pushed forward to within a mile of Cisterna. Facing an immovable enemy and having suffered 3,000 casualties since the landing on 22 January, General Truscott considered that his division had exhausted its offensive power and so decided to consolidate his troops on a defensible front, before the expected German counter-offensive opened.

The British advance

To the west, General Penney decided on a two-phase attack for his advance up the Via Anziate. In the first phase, 24 Guards Brigade would seize a track joining the main road one mile south of Campoleone Station as a start line for 3 Infantry Brigade. 1st Battalion of 6 (US) Armored Infantry Regiment would capture a section of railway line northwest of Carroceto as the American start line. In the second phase, 3 Infantry Brigade, supported by 46th RTR and 2nd, 19th and 24th Field, and 80th Medium Regiments RA, would pass through the Guards and take the road and rail crossing at Campoleone Station as the first objective and Osteriaccia as the second. On the American flank, Combat Command A of General Harmon's 1st (US) Armored Division was to cross the start line secured during the first phase, and then swing north-westwards to attack Campoleone from that direction.

Again, the detail of 1st Division's operations northwards from the Flyover is to be found elsewhere, in Chapter 2, and will not be considered here other than in very broad outline. The Division pushed up the Via Anziate almost to Campoleone Station before General Lucas halted it during the afternoon of 31 January.

The Allied advances thus far had achieved, on 1st Division's front, a salient jutting into enemy territory some 7,000 yards deep and 3,500 yards wide at the base. The apex was about 2,600 yards wide. To defend against the possibility that the Germans would attack the flanks of the salient General Penney ordered 3 Infantry Brigade to consolidate in its northern end, while 2 Infantry Brigade was brought up into positions southwest of Carroceto. 1st Reconnaisance Regiment and the Loyals covered the east flank. 1st (US) Armored Division was withdrawn into Corps' reserve. British casualties since 22 January now totalled 2,100, and 46th RTR had lost eleven Shermans. On 3rd (US) Division's front the Americans had pushed their line about one and a half miles forward, but neither Cisterna nor Campoleone had been taken.

General Alexander arrived in the beachhead on 31 January and stayed until 2 February. Unhappy with the failure of Lucas' attack, he toured the front visiting all senior commanders before ordering Clark to extend the left flank of the beachhead to the Incastro River and to make further efforts to take Cisterna and Campoleone, without which VI Corps would be unable to progress. As a precursor to a major offensive, the corps would temporarily go onto the defensive while improving lateral communications behind the front lines, so that there was improved freedom of movement for deploying reserves. Unaware of Alexander's orders at this time, Lucas instructed VI Corps to prepare for an expected German counterattack, which he believed to be imminent.

By 3 February the corps had received more – very welcome – reinforcements: the remainder of 45th (US) Division, the First Special Service Force, and 168 (British) Infantry Brigade. The last two of these formations had been moved from the Garigliano front.

The German attack

As recounted earlier, the Germans had been preparing an attack of their own. Von Mackensen had suspended this while he dealt with the Allied offensive, but now that this had stalled, he was ready to resume his own plans. Like the Allies, he had to carry out some reorganisation before he could attack. Indeed, much of the headquarters' activity on both sides involved commanders and staff officers in moving formations and units into different structures and locations in one attempt after another to find the right combination to further their aims, whether they were to block their enemy's attacks or to ensure that their own offensives succeeded.

The Germans had only two full-strength divisions (*26th Panzer Grenadier* and *715th Infantry Divisions*) available, and the less well-equipped *Hermann Göring Panzer* and *3rd Panzer Grenadier Divisions'* performances had not lived up to expectations. Furthermore, General Schlemm's command of the battle thus far had disappointed Kesselring. He therefore moved General Herr and his experienced *LXXVI Panzer Corps* Headquarters from *Tenth Army* to the Anzio front to take command of *3rd Panzer Grenadier*, *715th* and *71st Infantry*, the *Hermann Göring Panzer* and *26th Panzer Grenadier Divisions*. The

A German observation post on the Alban Hills. Every move that the Allies made was seen.

headquarters was based at Giulianello on the Velletri-Cori road. Headquarters *I Parachute Corps*, at Grottaferrata, kept *4th Parachute* and *65th Infantry Division*s under command.

On 28 January Hitler issued a directive to Kesselring, in which he stated that the impending 'Battle for Rome' (his words) would be decisive. If *Tenth Army*'s lines of communication were cut, he wrote, it would have to withdraw from the Gustav Line, and this in turn would decide the fate of the defence of central Italy, which was important to more than just the theatre itself. The Anzio landing was the beginning of the Allied invasion of Europe, and was designed to wear down German strength. German forces must therefore drive the Allies back into the sea. Von Mackensen was not sure that he could do this, however. The Allies had a strong force ashore, which was particularly well supported by artillery and an air force far superior to anything the *Luftwaffe* could put into the Italian skies. Having had to commit so many of his units to resisting the VI Corps' attack on 30 and 31 January, von Mackensen was in the process of regrouping before launching a general counter-offensive. While this continued, he proposed mounting a series of limited attacks to improve his front and to keep the Allies off-balance. The first of these attacks would be on the Campoleone salient on 3 February. Meanwhile, he pressed Kesselring for reinforcements. The *Fourteenth Army* units at Anzio were a mixed bunch, and von Mackensen required a first-class, well-equipped formation, preferably armoured, to give him some hope of success. Without further support, he could only attack if and when the tactical situation gave the opportunity.

Kesselring had the problem that the *Tenth Army* was heavily engaged at Cassino, and taking troops from there would be risky. If Cassino were to be held, more troops were needed, and so he moved *1st Parachute Division* there from the quiet Adriatic front. On 6 February Hitler summoned von Mackensen to give a personal report on the situation. Stating that he had established a firm defensive front, von Mackensen added that he could mount a counter-offensive to commence on or about 15 February. Hitler refused him a fresh division to assist in this. He did, however, agree to the transfer of the *Infantry Lehr Regiment* from Germany. *Infantry Lehr* was a prestigious demonstration unit, and in addition von Mackensen received some Tiger tanks and further weapons such as the *Sturmpanzer*, the *Goliath*, the

Jagdpanzer IV **issued to the** *Herman Göring Division* **in Italy in March 1944.**

Goliath controlled demolition vehicle.

Demolition Carrier, and the Elephant, all of which were new to the Italian theatre.

The German attacks were launched on 1 February. Elements of *71st Infantry*, *26th Panzer Grenadier* and *Hermann Göring Panzer Division*s made unsuccessful advances near Carano and Isola Bella. General Schlemm had planned to use *65th Infantry* and part of *3rd Panzer Grenadier Divisions* to attack the Campoleone sector that night, but Allied bombing wrecked the *Panzer Grenadier* artillery communications and stopped ammunition being brought up to the guns. The attack was consequently postponed until the night of 3/4 February. The plan was to isolate and then eliminate 3 Infantry Brigade at the point of the salient by having two battalions from *104 Panzer Grenadier Regiment* (attached to *3rd Panzer Grenadier Division*) attack westwards through Colle della Mandria to the railway line running from Anzio to Campoleone. Tufello was to be attacked from the west by two battalions of *145 Grenadier Regiment*, and from the southwest by two battalions of *147 Grenadier Regiment* (all from *65th Infantry Division*).

Heavy assault gun the Elfant, or Ferdinand

The operations to eliminate the salient are covered in Chapters 2 and 3, but may be summarised by stating that 1st

Division fought a grim battle to extricate 3 Brigade from the north, and then held the Factory area and Carroceto against overwhelming odds until it was forced to withdraw on 11 February.

1st Division had by now been reduced to half its effective strength, and it was necessary for the VI Corps' Commander to reorganize his troops. During the night of 9/10 February General Lucas replaced 2 Infantry Brigade with 180 Infantry Regiment from 45th (US) Division, in Corps reserve. At General Penney's request for reinforcements to mount an attack to drive the Germans out of Aprilia and Carroceto, and off the Buonriposo Ridge, Lucas moved 1st Battalion 179 Infantry and two companies of 191st Tank Battalion forward to relieve 3 Infantry Brigade, which itself took up positions extending from the Via Anziate to the southern end of Buonriposo Ridge. The Dukes sat astride the Via Anziate, with the KSLI and the Sherwood Foresters to their west. The Irish Guards were in the wadis south of Cava di Pozzolana. 2 Infantry Brigade moved back to the area around the Flyover, and 24 Guards Brigade and 168 Infantry Brigade to the Padiglioni Woods.

During the early morning of 11 February two companies of

German self-propelled gun and destroyed Allied and German armour in Carroceto.

1/179 Infantry and two companies of tanks attacked Aprilia unsuccessfully. At 1300 hours they tried again, got into the southern end of the town, but were driven out; two fresh companies renewed the attack at 0200 hours the following day, with the same result. The numbers of troops tasked with this mission were too few for them to have had any chance of success. The battle once again sank into a period of uneasy calm.

The lull allowed the Allies to reorganize, once again. General Alexander decided that the losses in 1st Division meant that the whole of 56th (British) Division should move up from the Garigliano to join 168 Brigade. The Divisional Commander, Major General GWR Templer, arrived on 12 February, followed by 167 Brigade the following day. The division's third brigade, 169, arrived on 13 February. The division took over the front from the coast, along the Moletta River to a point a mile west of the Via Anziate, via the Rione la Cagna, south of the Buonriposo Ridge. To its right was 45th (US) Division, stretching eastwards to Carano, where 3rd (US) Division held the line. The First Special Service Force linked their positions onwards to the sea.

Behind the scenes – the strategic view

It will be understood from the forgoing account that Operation SHINGLE had not turned out as the strategic planners had hoped. Unhappy with the progress of the war in Italy generally, and at Anzio specifically, the American Chiefs of Staff had worries that the campaign was becoming a battle of attrition without noticeable benefit to the war effort. On 4 February Sir John Dill reported this concern to the British Chiefs of Staff; two days later Churchill added his voice to those demanding an explanation, asking General Sir Henry Maitland Wilson to explain 'why no attempt had been made to occupy the high ground, and at least the towns of Velletri, Campoleone and Cisterna within twelve to twenty-four hours after the unopposed landing.' Wilson's reply stated that the delay was probably down to Lucas not grasping the importance of doing so, and that he probably suffered from a 'Salerno complex', that is, he expected a counterattack and that therefore he felt it necessary to prepare to deal with it rather than moving energetically inland. Furthermore, Wilson continued, Generals Alexander and Clark had visited the beachhead to push for an advance; no fault was found with their part in the conduct of operations. Churchill also asked Sir John Cunningham how many vehicles had been put ashore at Anzio by D+14. The answer was 17,940, which led Churchill to call into question the balance between fighting and support troops and materiel in VI Corps. He was unconvinced about the requirement for large numbers of logistic and administrative units to sustain the combat arms and seemed inclined to view transport problems in Italy as being no more difficult than he experienced when being driven around Britain; indeed, the result of his enquiry about the number of Anzio vehicles drew from him the barbed comment that 'we must have a great superiority of chauffeurs.' Churchill was continuing to play the military strategist.

General Marshall also weighed in, with a letter to General Devers (Wilson's American deputy) instructing him to ask Wilson if there was any criticism of American commanders – if so, they would be removed. Wilson's response was that the question would be better answered by Clark, to which came the

German troops moving through Cisterna.

reply that it might well be Clark who would be the one to be sacked. Wilson stated that he was satisfied not only with Clark, but also with Lucas, despite the fact that he might have done more initially. The matter did not rest there, however. Alexander and Clark had their own opinions, and they felt that Lucas was lacking. On 16 February Alexander told Clark that he was unhappy with Lucas' performance, and that he believed him to be too physically and mentally tired to keep up with the rapidly developing situation. Clark agreed.

Moving Lucas from command presented Clark with difficulties. He did not want to hurt the man who had done much for the Allied successes since Salerno. He therefore proposed appointing two Deputy Corps Commanders, Major General Truscott for the Americans, and Major General Evelegh for the British. Once the present fighting became less intense, Lucas would be replaced by Truscott. The preponderance of troops in the beachhead was American, and it was natural that command would go to them. Lucas was not to be demoted, however – rather the reverse. He would be appointed Deputy Commander Fifth Army. In fact, he would hold that appointment for only a short period. After three weeks there he was to move on to command the Fourth Army in the United States.

The main German attack – Operation 'FISCHFANG'
General von Mackensen began to concentrate on preparations for the offensive which would drive the Allies into the sea. From 9 February he and his senior generals, Herr and Schlemm, started to draw up plans for an infantry attack on the front between the Fosso di Spaccasassi on the east and the Buonriposo Ridge to the west. The initial phase of the operation, codenamed *FISCHFANG* (Catching Fish) would be to breach the Allied line in this sector, which would be followed by an infantry advance towards Nettuno. A wave of armour and motorised troops would either destroy Allied centres of resistance by flank attacks, or would drive straight through to Nettuno. The main role in this operation was to be taken by *LXXVI Panzer Corps* which would use *3rd Panzer Grenadier*, *715th Infantry*, and *114th Jäger Divisions*, with the *Infantry Lehr Regiment*, to break through the Allied line. The motorised troops would consist of *29th Panzer Grenadier* and *26th Panzer Divisions*,

The Flyover from the south. A number of tanks may be seen, one of which has been circled.

with *1st Battalion 4 Panzer Regiment*. The latter group would open the offensive with a diversionary attack near Cisterna, and then move westwards to take part in the main attack on the Via Anziate. This plan was later changed to give the diversionary role to the *Hermann Göring Panzer Division*, which would have Isola Bella as its objective. *I Parachute Corps* would protect the right flank of *LXXVI Panzer Corps*. The odds for this operation, as calculated by Kesselring, were that the Allies had five more battalions than he, if he included only his 'battle-worthy' ones in the reckoning. The Allies had superior numbers of tanks, artillery pieces and aircraft; but these figures did not lower the German commanders' morale. They were optimistic of success.

German tactics were changed to cater for the conditions. Tanks would no longer lead well to the front of the attack, because of the Allied anti-tank guns and mines; they would advance alongside the infantry and more cooperation between the two arms would be called for. Hitler also dictated from afar that the best tanks would not be exposed recklessly. The artillery would not expend its limited ammunition stocks in barrages, but would be used for closely targeted counterbattery missions and observed fire to break up enemy concentrations.

The operation was timetabled to commence at 0630 hours on 16 February. Despite the Allies having dropped over 700 tons of bombs during the previous three days, the Germans were able to start the battle as scheduled. Counterbattery artillery bombardments opened the action, and the *Hermann Göring Diversion* succeeded in gaining about 1,000 yards of ground near Ponte Rotto. On the Via Anziate *3rd Panzer Grenadier Division* forced its way through some of 45th (US) Division's positions and advanced about a mile, but no further. To their east, *715th Infantry Division* did the same. West of these attacks, elements of *4th Parachute* and *65th Infantry Division*s got into 167 Brigade's positions but failed to break through. On the Via Anziate *Infantry Lehr*, the prestigious demonstration unit, broke under artillery fire and fled.

During the day's fighting the Germans had found it difficult to make best use of their tanks because of the softness of the ground, which made off-road travel impossible. They also suffered some 174 tons of bombs dropped on the battlefield by Allied aircraft during the hours of daylight; and after dark Wellington and Boston bombers continued to attack them. The Allied line held.

Throughout the night the Germans continued their attempts to infiltrate the Allied positions. Von Mackensen set the road running from S. Lorenzo to Padiglioni as the objective for the following day, and ordered Generals Herr and Schlemm to push on towards it. As yet, he did not consider that the time had come to commit *29th Panzer Grenadier* and *26th Panzer Divisions*, as the Allied front had not been broken. The Germans forced a gap between 2/157 Infantry who were astride the Via Anziate and 2/179th Infantry to the east. On 17 February this gap was exploited by *3rd Panzer Grenadier Division* and *715th Infantry Division*, who pushed about a mile deep on a front of two and a half miles by midday. Constant German attacks, where one battalion followed another in an attempt to maintain the momentum, were fiercely resisted by 167 Brigade and 45th (US) Division, with the support of almost all of the artillery in the beachhead. Another 833 tons of bombs were also dropped on the attackers during the day, with a further ninety-five tons that night, the largest amount of air support for a single day thus far given in the Mediterranean.

On 17 February General Lucas ordered 1st Division, less 3 Brigade which he held back in reserve, to occupy the section of the Corps' final defence line on either side of the Flyover. He also ordered Major General Eagles, commander of 45th (US) Division, to make a counterattack to restore the situation on 179

German paratroops on the Moletta River.

Infantry's front. To assist him in this, Lucas reinforced the division with an extra battalion of infantry.

After midday on the same day General Truscott moved to Corps Headquarters as Deputy Commander. There he found Lucas in pessimistic mood, which he compared with the more positive attitude displayed by Eagles and Harmon. He felt that Lucas and his staff tended to rely on second-hand reports and give them the most discouraging interpretation, when they could have been out on the ground seeing for themselves that the situation was not as bad as it had been conjured up in their imaginations.

German pressure continued throughout the night of 17/18 February, and von Mackensen threw *26th Panzer* and *29th Panzer Grenadier Division*s into the battle on the 18th. The S. Lorenzo-Padiglione road, the objective for the 17th, had not been taken, and the German casualties (from an incomplete return) for 16 and 17 February were estimated at 2,569. Some battalions were down to a maximum of 150 effective men, heavy losses having been inflicted mostly by the Allied artillery, which fired some 158,000 rounds over the period 17-20 February. Nonetheless, von Mackensen was relatively content with what had been achieved.

715th Infantry Division infiltrated between 179 and 180 Infantry Regiments to the east of Via Anziate during the night.

German armoured car and paratroops.

Infantry and Panther tank. The state of the ground is not conducive to armoured warfare.

On the western side of the road, 2/157 Infantry became surrounded by parts of *65th Infantry* and *4th Parachute Division*s. Isolated in the wadis and caves at the southern end of the Buonriposo Ridge, the battalion held out until it was relieved by 2/7th Queens Regiment on the night of 21/22 February. From a strength of 800 men, it was reduced to 225, but the stand made by the battalion prevented the Germans from cutting into the Allied positions from the west.

The Germans were not the only ones attacking that night. General Eagles counterattacked to retrieve the ground lost on 179 Infantry Regiment's front. 2/ and 3/179 Infantry Regiment and 191st Tank Battalion attacked to the east of Via Anziate, while 3/157 Infantry advanced up it. By this time, however, the Germans had consolidated on their gains and were able to repel the attack.

On the Corps' main line of resistance 2 Infantry Brigade had occupied the Flyover area. 6th Gordons were west of the Flyover, with the Loyals to their east and the North Staffordshires in reserve. 24 Guards Brigade was echeloned back on the left rear of 2 Brigade to give depth and to protect the west flank. At dawn on 18 February *I Parachute Corps* and *LXXVI Panzer Corps* attempted once again to reach the S. Lorenzo-Padiglione road. *67 Panzer Grenadier Regiment* came down the Via Anziate, with *15 Panzer Grenadier Regiment* to the east of the road advancing onto the *715 Infantry Regiment's* positions. *I Parachute Corps* continued fighting, but without gaining advantage, on the southern end of Buonriposo Ridge.

East of the Via Anziate *114th Jäger* and *3rd Panzer Grenadier* Divisions, and *67* and *15 Panzer Grenadier Regiments*, struck hard, the main attack falling on the Loyals' positions. The Germans may have hoped to take advantage of the weakened state of 715 Infantry Regiment following their failed attack earlier, but the Loyals and their American comrades on their right held firm. The Loyals mounted an immediate counterattack to restore the situation; a more detailed account of their action may be found in Chapter 3. The artillery laid on five concentrated shoots which caused very heavy casualties in the enemy ranks, but bad weather grounded the bombers. That evening the most advanced Germans were just north of the S. Lorenzo-Padiglione road, and that – apart from a brief spell on 19 February – was as far as they were going to get.

General Truscott believed that VI Corps still had potential, despite the pervading air of despondency in Headquarters. 169 Infantry Brigade had landed during the morning of 18 February, with other assets with which the Corps could mount a counterattack. Truscott argued for this, supported by Clark who was making one of his visits to the beachhead. Lucas agreed to a converging attack in which 6 Armored Infantry Regiment (minus one battalion) and a battalion of Shermans from 1st (US) Armored Division, and 30 Infantry Regiment from 3rd (US) Division advanced along the Padiglione-Carroceto road while 169 Infantry Brigade moved up the Via Anziate. The objective was the 'Dead End Road' which was some 1,500 yards north of the S. Lorenzo-Padiglione road.

General Lucian Truscott

169 Brigade's advance failed to materialise, however, because German aircraft had mined Anzio harbour, creating problems in offloading their equipment from the transports. The American

58

force commenced its advance at 0630 hours on 19 February and caught the Germans off-guard. With their signals system wrecked by Allied bombing, they were unable to coordinate their activities; in any event, the steam was fast running out of their attack. *3rd Panzer Grenadier* and *26th Panzer Divisions* had tried to resume their offensive on the Via Anziate early on 19 February but made no progress in the face of Allied artillery fire. To their east *1st* and *3rd Battalions* of *15 Panzer Grenadier Regiment* were close to extinction. In the wadis south of Buonriposo Ridge *I Parachute Corps* was making no progress either.

General Harmon's advance up the Padiglione-Carroceto road reached its objective in the early afternoon. 2 Infantry Brigade seized its opportunity, and the Loyals, North Staffordshires and a squadron of tanks from 46th RTR pushed up the Via Anziate for about a mile.

The German offensive had been defeated. Kesselring proposed suspending it for the time being, and Hitler agreed. *Fourteenth Army* would regroup and prepare another attack further east, and on a broader front than *FISCHFANG*. VI Corps had experienced little difficulty in identifying the German line of attack – indeed, it had not been hard, given the problems both sides were experiencing in deploying armour off-road in the current weather conditions – and were prepared,

Major General EN Harmon, commander 1st (US) Armored Division.

particularly with superior artillery and air power, to counter any German moves down the obvious route to Anzio. The Germans were now facing a similar problem to that experienced by the Allies a few days before: they were in an exposed salient which they would have difficulty enlarging or defending. Furthermore, they had lost 5,389 men in the period from 16 to 20 February in attempting to break through to the coast. Nonetheless, if the Germans were not to continue fighting on both the Anzio and Gustav Line fronts, then VI Corps would have to be pushed into the sea at some stage.

Apart from local battles on the shoulders of the German salient, in the wadis and to the east of Via Anziate, the fighting died down between 20-29 February. *Fourteenth Army* was reorganising, while VI Corps changed commander as Truscott replaced Lucas on 22 February. Two days later 18 Infantry Brigade arrived at Anzio, detached from 1st (British) Armoured Division.

At this stage the Allies gave up any hope of achieving an immediate success at Anzio. The emphasis now changed to ensuring that the beachhead was secure enough to exist for an indeterminate period. General Alexander began making plans for the conduct of the Italian campaign which involved moving most of the Eighth Army to the west coast to provide the local three-to-one superiority which was necessary for success. This could not be achieved until April. Meanwhile, pressure was to be kept up on the Germans so that they did not have the opportunity to move troops from the Mediterranean to France in time to resist OVERLORD. For the immediate future, the plan would be to defend Anzio and to attack at Cassino.

General Truscott

General Truscott's assumption of command of VI Corps brought a different style of leadership. Lucas had run operations from his headquarters and relied on reports to give him information, with which he chaired unstructured conferences that resulted in equally unstructured orders. He also found it difficult to

Truscott with 'Iron Mike' O'Daniel, who took over as commander 3rd Division.

develop good relationships with the British officers in the corps. Truscott's approach was radically different.

Truscott had started his working life as a schoolteacher, but joined the US Army during the First World War. He saw no active service during that conflict, but in the inter-war years he came to the attention of General Marshall as a promising officer. As a member of the Army polo team, Truscott displayed a fearlessness and drive to win that was to continue onto the battlefield. Having reached the rank of brigadier general, he was posted to Combined Service Headquarters in London where, with William O Darby, he helped form the Rangers. He was an observer during the Dieppe Raid, and took part in other amphibious operations before helping plan Operation TORCH. In March 1943 he was given command of the 3rd (US) Division, which he raised to a high level of fitness through a stiff training regime. The division became known for its ability to march faster, when fully loaded with equipment, than any other – the 'Truscott trot' was paced at five miles per hour rather than two and one-half, which was the standard US Army marching speed. This ability was to prove itself in Sicily.

Truscott inspired strong personal loyalty and generated the best from his men. He spent time visiting all parts of the beachhead, seeing and being seen. His previous experience of working on the staff in London gave him a good understanding of British procedures, and led to an improved relationship with that nation's officers and soldiers. He also radiated a positive dynamism, issuing clear and decisive orders, both of which characteristics led to increased morale.

Renewed German offensives

As mentioned above, the Germans were reorganising in preparation for another offensive. Their original intention was to launch it on or about 26 February, and Kesselring's plan was to use *LXXVI Panzer Corps* to push through the Allied line between Ponte della Crocetta and Isola Bella, aiming for the northern edge of the Padiglione woods. Hitler decreed, however, that this line of advance was too close to the one that had been used during *FISCHFANG*, and the attack should take place between the Astura River and the Mussolini Canal, where he believed (from his viewpoint in Berlin) that tanks could operate. An attack here would draw Allied troops away from the Campo di Carne area, leaving it open for a strike through to Nettuno. Kesselring and von Mackensen had little choice but to fall in line and revise their plans to comply with Hitler's tactics. Churchill was not the only political leader who considered himself to have a military talent.

The reorganisation was delayed for three days while *I Parachute Corps* finished clearing the Buonriposo Ridge. Von Mackensen moved *362nd Infantry Division* to *LXXVI Panzer Corps* from its positions on the coast north of the River Tiber, which gave him a fresh division. *3rd Panzer Grenadier Division* was moved from *LXXVI Panzer Corps* and placed under command of *I Parachute Corps*, which meant that *LXXVI Corps* was cleared of any responsibility for the Via Anziate sector and could concentrate on the forthcoming attack to the east. Both *26th Panzer* and *715th Infantry Division*s were moved from this area. For the new offensive von Mackensen would use *362nd Infantry Division* on the west, *26th Panzer Division* in the centre, and the *Hermann Göring Panzer Division* on the east.

Von Mackensen's aim was to break through southwest of Cisterna and to form bridgeheads over the River Astura southwest of Conca. The *Hermann Göring Panzer Division* would advance through Isola Bella and *26th Panzer Division* west of Ponte Rotto, starting at 0400 hours. To enhance the chance of surprise, a preparatory artillery barrage would not be fired before this attack, but one was to be used to clear the way for *362nd Infantry Division* when it advanced to Colle dei Pozzi and then Ponte della Crocetta at 0530 hours, by which time there was no advantage to be gained by not using it. The three divisions would aim to penetrate Allied lines on a front of about five miles wide and seven deep. Deception measures included having *I Parachute Corps* simulate an assembly area at Ardea and mount a minor attack in the Buonriposo area, while *LXXVI Panzer Corps* made a demonstration near Sessano on the eastern flank.

Planned to start on 28 February, the offensive was delayed until the following day because of bad weather on the 26th and 27th. Allied air superiority also meant that the Germans could only move at night, although the weather had grounded most bombing missions. Air observation aircraft, however, working at low altitudes and from a local airstrip, were able to maintain flying operations, and their presence gave the Germans the

Tiger destroyed near Cisterna.

impression that every movement was seen. The heavy rain led the Germans to adjust their plan to make best use of the roads for their armour. The road running from Spaccasassi to Campomorto through Carano and Ponte della Crocetta was to be brought into use, and *114th Jäger Division* was to capture Carano before *362nd Infantry Division* started their attack, and then join them in moving on Ponte della Crocetta.

Meanwhile VI Corps had improved its defences. The divisions which had been involved in the earlier fighting had been weakened by casualties and insufficient reinforcements, and there was the problem that many of the survivors were exhausted. General Truscott shuffled his forces around the front so that some units were able to take a short rest. From air observation reports he was able to forecast that the Germans were likely to strike southwest of Cisterna, where 3rd (US) Division was now positioned. An intercepted German message also gave the date of the offensive: 29 February. Truscott also suspected that the enemy would mount a diversionary attack down the Via Anziate. He therefore ordered his artillery to prepare a programme targeted on probable enemy assembly areas, reserve positions and gun batteries. This was to commence at 0430 hours on the day of the attack.

The main German attack on 3rd (US) Division started on time, and as planned. A heavy artillery bombardment accompanied the assault – the Germans fired 1,183 tons of shells during the day – which VI Corps replied to, although the Allied fire appears to have come too late to catch the enemy as they formed up for the assault. Nowhere, however, did the Germans succeed in denting the defences. *114th Jäger Division* failed to capture Carano, *362nd Infantry Division* was brought to a halt at Colle dei Pozzi, and *1st Battalion 955 Grenadier Regiment* got no closer than 300 yards short of Ponte della Crocetta. The same story of limited – or no – success was to be repeated everywhere on this section of the front. The mud, once again, proved too much for the tanks. They were generally restricted to the Velletri-Cisterna-Ponte Rotto road and played little part in the battle.

The diversionary action by *715th Infantry Division* on the eastern flank also came to nothing; and on the western edge of the battle area *I Parachute Corps'* infiltration of the wadis between 28 February and 1 March was described by the British Official History as 'almost a private war of singular beastliness' which produced no change to the line.

The weather closed in again and rain fell throughout the night of 29 February/1 March and the following day. All German vehicles were brought to a standstill. 3rd (US) Division mounted local counterattacks whenever and wherever the opportunity presented itself, and at 1840 hours on 1 March Kesselring brought the offensive to an end. The Germans had taken over 2,700 casualties, with no gains to show for these losses.

Stalemate

On 2 March the weather cleared and the air forces emerged from their time off. Bombers dropped 349 tons of fragmentation bombs around and between Cisterna and Velletri, another sixty tons near Cisterna and thirty-one tons near Carroceto, and forty-four tons on Campoleone and Velletri. Eighty-two tons were dropped across the VI Corps' front and along the Albano-Genzano road by 260 fighter-bombers. The next day the weather was less favourable, but Allied aircraft managed to drop another forty-three tons. The total weight of bombs dropped by the Middle East Air Force in support of the beachhead since 1

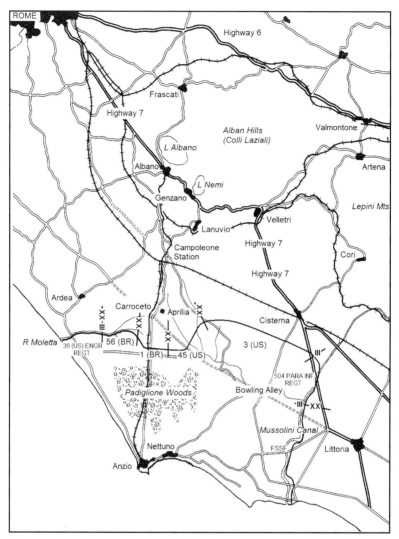

Stalemate.

February now came to 4,804 tons. Again, the raw statistics demonstrated the Allied ability to use the air without hindrance to inflict serious damage on the enemy – when the weather permitted.

From 22 January until 3 March the British suffered some 10,168 battle casualties and 3,860 sick; the Americans about 10,775 battle casualties. Incomplete returns for the Germans

65

218-ton German railway gun. Two of these, known as Leopold and Robert to the Germans and Anzio Annie and the Anzio Express to the Allies, could fire 280-mm shells a distance of thirty-six miles, and had the whole of the beachhead and much of the offshore unloading area within range.
They were notoriously difficult to pinpoint and bomb because of their mobility.

The harbour under fire.

were 10,306 battle casualties, but these may well have been higher. Both sides now ran down operations to draw breath before they joined in the final battle.

There were no large-scale operations from 3 March until the Allies broke out of the Anzio beachhead in May. On 13 and 14 March 18 Infantry Brigade, from 1st (British) Division made an unsuccessful attempt to drive the enemy from positions in the Wadi Caronte. 509th (US) Parachute Battalion made a raid near Carano on 15 March, and attempts were made by 17 Infantry Brigade from 5th (British) Division to improve their positions in the wadis on 19 March, but without significant result.

Once again, the opportunity arose for the generals to regroup and reorganise their forces. General Alexander was working towards a major offensive in the spring, and wanted to relieve some of the pressure on troops in the Anzio beachhead. To this end he moved 5th (British) Division up to Anzio from the Garigliano front, and 56th (British) Division left to go to Egypt. 24 Guards Brigade went to Naples, to be replaced in 1st (British) Division by 18 Infantry Brigade. For the Americans, 504 Parachute Infantry Regiment left for the United Kingdom to join 82nd Airborne Division and to prepare for Normandy, while 34th (US) Division arrived in Anzio from Naples. The net effect of these moves was that VI Corps now comprised five infantry and one armoured division, less one combat command.

Life in the beachhead assumed a pattern of no movement near the front lines during the hours of daylight – it was too dangerous, for snipers and artillery observers were ever vigilant. At night the beachhead came alive as troops resumed their patrolling and mine-laying, repaired their positions and resupplied them, and continued doing the myriad of tasks that were necessary to sustain life. Units and sub-units rotated through positions, the wounded were evacuated and the dead buried. Loads were transported to the forward posts by porters, struggling to find their way in the dark and harassed by random shell- and mortar-fire, machinegun bursts and flares. It was, at best, an unpleasant existence, and all too often a deadly one. At Anzio there were no safe areas. Everything was within range of the German gunners, and military policemen manned checkpoints to ensure that vehicles kept to speeds that were low enough to avoid raising tell-tale clouds of dust which would invite a 'stonk'. Some units avoided being close to crossroads on

The effect of air and artillery bombardment on Anzio town.

the quarter-hour, in the belief that enemy standing orders – true to the Germanic approach to life – dictated that they should be subjected to artillery fire according to a strict timetable.

Life in the beachhead was not entirely without relief, however. Units were rotated away from the front lines for rest and training, and battle-schools were set up to improve various military skills, such as the use of the hand grenade. Recreational activities – soccer, baseball, bathing and fishing with explosives, for example – took place. A particular attraction on the football field was a Swazi Pioneer known (in those less politically correct days) as 'Shoe-shine', whose cheerful appearance and skill drew crowds of spectators, buoyed up by the belief that whenever he was playing, the field would not be shelled. The American divisional bands gave concerts, there was the occasional visit by entertainers (Bob Hope and a USO troupe amongst them), and soldiers organised beetle races where heavy bets were laid. They also argued about which alcoholic drink was the worse:

Egyptian rum or Cypriot brandy. The consensus of opinion appeared to be that the only way to drink either was to take a swig of one, closely followed by a swig of the second, to take away the taste of the first.

The beachhead, of course, was still wholly reliant upon resupply by sea. In February some 62,048 tons of cargo were landed, a figure which rose to 157,173 tons in March. This latter figure represented an average daily amount of over 5,000 tons. The resupply had to contend with bad weather, German nuisance air-raids, and artillery fire. The problem of LST availability arose again in early March. To maintain the beachhead, Alexander's staff calculated that 2,700 tons were needed each day. To build up the force for future operations the requirement would be for 3,200 tons daily for maintenance and a further 800 tons for reserves. But the LSTs had a pressing engagement elsewhere – for OVERLORD. Thirteen British LSTs were to leave the Mediterranean on 29 February, and another twenty-eight on 1 April. Without them, the plans for building up the Anzio force would come to nothing.

On 29 February the First Sea Lord took responsibility for ordering a delay of forty-eight hours in returning the first group of LSTs to the United Kingdom, while the British Chiefs of Staff presented the case for retention to the Combined Chiefs. They proposed that twenty-six American LSTs, which were to have

American troops disembarking in Anzio harbour.

sailed to the Mediterranean later, would be diverted straight to England, while a similar number of British vessels stayed in the Mediterranean, available for immediate use. Such a solution was not as straightforward as might be imagined, however. In matters of international relations and of differing agendas, they rarely are. Lengthy negotiations involving sailing times, crew training, refurbishment of ships, and a multitude of other factors were discussed, and on 10 March a workable solution was found whereby thirteen British LSTs would stay for the time being, but they had to be in England on 11 May. Another twenty-eight were to refit in the Mediterranean and sail to be in England by 1 May. Twenty-six LSTs would sail from America to be in the Mediterranean by 10 April. This complicated arrangement was due, in part, to the fact that ships equipped for Mediterranean conditions were unsuitable for the Channel waters, and vice-versa. It all seemed unnecessarily complicated, but doubtless the strategists and the naval experts knew what they were talking about.

A further factor to add to the resupply problem was the bi-national composition of VI Corps. For many items of equipment, ammunition types, and even food the American and British requirements were different; for others, such as petrol, the Americans supplied all units in the beachhead, which consumed 60,000 gallons a day despite the fact that all movement was being done in a comparatively small area and mostly only during the hours of darkness. On 13 March the numbers of vehicles at Anzio, including tanks, half-tracks and artillery tractors came to 24,234. The beachhead was becoming increasingly choked.

On the German side, post-operational analysis of the battles thus far put the reason for the failure to drive the Allies into the sea down to the inexperience of many of the troops, and of their units, and also to the Allied artillery and air power. Many of the Germans overestimated the Allies, and there was a general shortage of seasoned officers and NCOs with the knowledge and experience to correct this belief; the result, for some units, was a loss of confidence. If the Germans were to succeed, they needed two battle-hardened divisions to stiffen up *Fourteenth Army*.

Appeals to Hitler failed to produce the required divisions. Kesselring was told to restructure and retrain his current force, and *Fourteenth Army* was (at least in principle) to keep to its aim of throwing the Allies off the beachhead. Regrouping was necessary: the Fifth Army, on the Gustav Line, was now stronger than the German *Tenth Army*, opposing it; the Germans might expect the Allies to attempt further landings on the exposed Italian coastline, possibly at Civitavecchia or even Genoa; but, on the more positive side, it appeared that VI Corps was not yet in a position to effect a major breakout. Consequently the *Hermann Göring Panzer Division* was to leave *Fourteenth Army* and redeploy to Lucca to act as a reserve in case of another landing, and *114th Jäger Division* was to go to *Tenth Army* to reinforce the Gustav Line. *26th Panzer Division* and *29th Panzer Grenadier Division* were to leave the line at Anzio to form the *Fourteenth Army* Reserve. This restructuring left *LXXVI Panzer Corps* with only *362nd* and *715th Infantry Division*s. But because the weather made armoured operations impossible until the ground dried in the Spring, the Germans would restrict their activities to active defence – raids and patrols – while preparing for any attack by the Allies. Various plans which *Fourteenth Army* Headquarters drew up for attacking the beachhead came to nothing because the Germans could not assemble enough artillery ammunition to support the operations, partly because of the Allied air forces' disruption of the lines of communication. Neither side could raise the strength to mount an offensive at Anzio.

The breakthrough and breakout plans

On 22 February General Alexander submitted an appreciation of the situation to General Wilson, written by his Chief of Staff, Lieutenant General AF Harding. In it, he stated his objective as being 'To force the enemy to commit the maximum number of divisions to operations in Italy at the time OVERLORD is launched.' Although he was unaware of the detailed timing for the Normandy landings, he assumed that he had relatively little time to achieve his aim, operations for which purpose must be underway at least two or three weeks before OVERLORD. With only one fresh formation, 78th (British) Division, in hand, and 88th (US) Division expected to arrive in Italy in early March, reorganisation was necessary to refresh the remainder and to bring them up to strength. He therefore proposed a period of inactivity once the current period of fighting at Cassino (the

Third Battle of Cassino was to extend from 15 to 23 March 1944) died down. Such a lull would be possible because enemy losses, exhaustion and lack of reinforcements and supplies made it unlikely that they could go onto the offensive.

For an attack to succeed, a local superiority of three to one in infantry was required in the Italian terrain, and it should take place where full advantage of Allied artillery dominance would take effect. This pointed to the Liri Valley, the route to Rome blocked by Cassino, where the New Zealand Corps had been fighting itself to a standstill. Cassino and Anzio were inextricably linked: as the lynchpin of the Gustav Line, Cassino had to fall if VI Corps was to be relieved; the reason for SHINGLE had been to split the German defences so that the Gustav Line could be breached.

During the lull in offensive operations Fifth and Eighth Armies would be restructured. There would be two corps, each of three infantry and one armoured divisions, to make the breach in the Gustav Line; and two corps, each of two infantry and a single armoured division, to exploit the breakthrough. To remove the administrative problems of having American and British units in the same corps (as illustrated by the supply difficulties at Anzio), American-equipped formations would serve together as would British-equipped ones. Fifth Army would therefore comprise American and French formations, Eighth Army would be made up of British, Commonwealth and Polish ones.

As far as Anzio was concerned, the Allied presence there threatened *Tenth Army*'s lines of communication, and if the Germans kept attacking the beachhead they would continue to run down their forces by losing men and materiel. Furthermore, if VI Corps could be built up and a stockpile of supplies created, then a force of three or four divisions could strike towards Valmontone to coincide with an advance up the Liri Valley from Cassino; this would give the Allies the opportunity to cut off and destroy *Tenth Army* units withdrawing westwards on Highway 6 once the Gustav Line had been broken open.

Alexander's plan was for a corps consisting of three divisions to take over Eighth Army's front on the Adriatic, in a defensive role. Eighth Army itself would clear Cassino and establish a bridgehead across the Rapido River, before driving up Highway 6 – the Liri Valley.

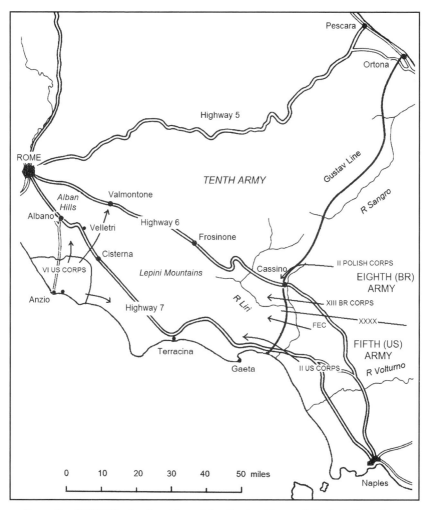

Operation DIADEM – the breaking of the Gustav Line and the isolation of the Tenth Army.

Fifth Army was to advance along the southern coastal road, supported by an amphibious operation in the Gaeta area, and through the mountains south of the Liri. VI Corps was to take Cisterna and Carroceto and advance on Velletri and Valmontone to block the withdrawal of *Tenth Army*.

Preparation for all of this would take time; reorganising formations along national lines was not merely a matter of shifting all British units to the Eighth Army. For example, the entire logistic 'tail' had to be restructured, together with new allocations of lines of communication, repositioning stocks of equipment, ammunition, and so on; it was not expected that the entire process would be complete before 23 April. Once a 'fudge factor' had been added to cater for unexpected delays, the date for opening the battle came to 3-5 May. This fell in line with the requirement to open the offensive before OVERLORD to maximise its purpose of tying German forces down, well away from Normandy.

Discussion then turned to whether it should be the breakout from Anzio that came before the breach of the Gustav Line, or vice-versa. Alexander's initial proposal was for VI Corps to break out, and then pause while the Fifth and Eighth Armies fought their way through the Gustav Line. Mounting a simultaneous attack at Anzio and on the Gustav Line raised the problem that air support would have to be split between the two fronts. For the breakout from Anzio to precede the Gustav Line attack, there would have to be more certainty that the German line surrounding the beachhead could be breached; if not, then VI Corps' offensive would not get off the ground. The final decision was that the main assault would start first, and that VI Corps would be on twenty-four hours' notice to move with

A Browning machine gun position at Anzio.

effect from D+4. D-Day for Fifth and Eighth Armies was set for 11 May 1944, with H-Hour at 2300 hours.

To draw enemy forces away from the key areas, a deception plan was put into operation. With only enough vessels to land a single division, the Allies could not mount another SHINGLE-type operation deep behind German lines. However, the possibility of this happening was to be skilfully engineered to give the Germans the impression that a major landing was being planned at Civitavecchia. A force was assembled in the Salerno area which purported to be I Canadian Corps and 36th (US) Division. With the aid of dummy wireless messages and the use of maple leaves and other Canadian insignia on signposts and vehicles, the impression was given that the Canadians were preparing a landing. Air reconnaissance was heavy over Civitavecchia, and German radar stations in the area were targeted by bombers, all of which activity was designed to add to the deception. Meanwhile, I Canadian Corps – without its vehicles being adorned by the maple leaf – was concentrating behind XIII Corps on the Gari River, preparing to follow through once the Gustav Line had been broken. The false messages and dummy rehearsals also gave the impression that the offensive would be launched during the second half of May.

German intelligence was confused as a result of the Allied deception measures. General von Vietinghoff, commander of *Tenth Army*, believed that Allied movements represented a series of reliefs to pave the way for Fifth Army to link up with VI Corps, probably assisted by landings from the sea which would outflank the Germans. A resumption of attacks at Cassino seemed unlikely, indeed, the Germans believed that the position there had proved to be so strong that the Allies would now concentrate on the coast and would try to roll up the *Tenth Army* positions from there. Not expecting the offensive to commence until the latter half of May, the Germans began to relax. On 17 April, General von Senger, commanding *XIV Panzer Corps* which defended the southern end of the Gustav Line between the Liri Valley and the Tyrrhenian Sea, went on leave. On 11 May, the day that the Allies launched their offensive, von Vietinghoff departed for Hitler's headquarters to receive a decoration. Once again, the German intelligence services had failed them.

Breaking the Gustav Line

The attack on the Gustav Line opened at 2300 hours on 11 May, with an artillery barrage delivered by some 2,000 guns. After six days of fighting Cassino fell, and the way up the Liri Valley, Highway 6, was open. Although the Germans strongly resisted the advance, the Poles in the mountains to the north and the French drive through the Aurunci Mountains south of the valley sealed the matter. The newly-constructed German defence line, the Hitler Line, was outflanked and rendered obsolete. It was promptly renamed the Senger Line to salvage the Führer's pride.

The Germans had been caught out. Kesselring had interpreted the attacks on the Gustav Line as being a feint to draw his reserves south, away from another landing site, or possibly to enable a breakout from Anzio. The deception plan had worked; the Canadian Corps which was believed to be in the Naples area ready for embarkation suddenly appeared in front of them, and the French penetration was too deep to be countered. It was not until aerial reconnaissance failed to find an Allied invasion fleet sailing up the coast that *26th Panzer Division* was ordered south to shore up the faltering line. As the Allied advance pressed onwards, Kesselring ordered *29th*

A German prisoner is interrogated by an American officer and a sergeant from 78th Infantry Division, which was part of the force which broke the Gustav Line.

The builup continues in preparation for the breakout from the beachhead.

Panzer Division, his last reserve in the Rome area, to take up positions between Fondi and Terracina to halt the Allied advance along the south coast. Von Mackensen disagreed, and the delay in implementing the order allowed the Americans to occupy the high ground before the Germans arrived. The time for VI Corps to break out had come.

Since early March 1944 the situation at Anzio had been one of stalemate, while both sides worked to improve their positions and to prepare their forces for the battle that they knew must come. On the Allied side, the corps had been reinforced and now consisted of seven full divisions (one of them armoured), the First Special Service Force, and various supporting units. The artillery component was particularly powerful, with twenty-nine American field artillery battalions and three howitzer batteries, and two British medium and seven field regiments.

General Clark had given Truscott the task of preparing the plans for the breakout towards Valmontone which Alexander had outlined. Three plans were drawn up by VI Corps staff: BUFFALO, for the thrust to Valmontone; TURTLE, for an attack further west, along the axis Carroceto-Campoleone-Rome; and

CRAWDAD, for a move through Ardea to Rome. The last two of these were developed to turn the German lines in the event that they made a quick withdrawal into positions in the Alban Hills. However, during a visit to Anzio Alexander left Truscott in no doubt that his task was to cut Highway 6 at Valmontone; there was only one direction in which VI Corps should move. Clark regarded this as interference in the American chain of command.

General Truscott's BUFFALO plan was, firstly, to take a bite out of the German lines (known as the X-Y Line) stretching from four miles east to four miles west of Cisterna, and about two miles deep. The central attacking force was to be 3rd (US) Division, flanked by First Special Service Force to the east and 1st (US) Armored and then 45th (US) Division on the west. The second phase was for 36th (US) Division to pass through 3rd Division and move north-westwards through Cori, while the armour advanced to a line between Giulianello and Velletri and First Special Service Force to Monte Arrestino. Then 1st (US) Armored, 3rd (US) and 36th (US) Divisions would unite to take Artena. Further moves to capture Valmontone would depend on how things went at Artena.

The British Divisions in the beachhead (1st and 5th) were tasked with holding their current positions on the west and to engage the enemy through aggressive patrolling. Localised diversionary attacks were to be mounted to further occupy the Germans.

The German preparations for dealing with a breakout were based on the assumption that the Allied move would – yet again – be focused on the Via Anziate, which had been the route to and from Anzio that had been the axis for most of the advances made by both sides since January. As we have seen, the reason for this choice had been that the off-road going had been too wet for tanks; but now there had been a dry period and other routes were possible.

German dispositions, running clockwise around the beachhead, were *I Parachute Corps* (*4th Parachute*, *65th Infantry* and *3rd Panzer Grenadier Divisions*) to the west, running along the Moletta River, astride the Via Anziate and to the north of Carano; and *LXXVI Panzer Corps* (*362nd Infantry* and *715th Infantry Divisions*) in and around Cisterna and along the Mussolini Canal. Five German divisions faced the Allied strength of over seven. Von Mackensen deployed his most

The overwhelming superiority of the Allied air forces was a potent factor in the battle. Route 7 is bombed.

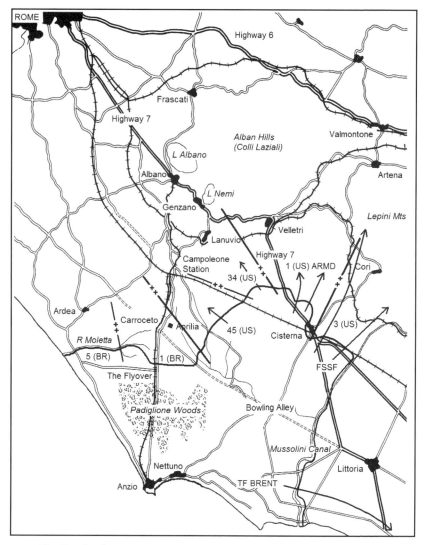

The Breakout.

experienced divisions on the Via Anziate.

To strengthen the defences of Rome, the Germans firmed-up another resistance line, the Caesar Line (also known as the C-Line), which crossed Highways 6 and 7 between Anzio and Rome running through Avezzano to points west of Pescaro. German engineers and 10,000 Italian labourers had completed the line to about two miles north of Valmontone, but thereafter it was no more than a façade.

Germans inspecting a destroyed Sherman.

On 19 May, General Alexander signalled that VI Corps' operations to break out from the beachhead would start either during the night of 21/22 May, or on the latter day. This timetable slipped by a day to optimise coordination with the advance up the Liri Valley, and the Anzio breakout operation started with 1st and 5th (British) Divisions, now detached from VI Corps and directly under Fifth Army command, carrying out their diversionary attacks to strengthen the German belief that the main thrust would be in the western beachhead and on the Via Anziate. Facing 5th Division was the German *4th Parachute Division*, behind mines and wire stretching inland from the coast. 1st Battalion, The Green Howards mounted a battalion-sized raid towards the town of L'Americano, across the Moletta River, supported by the divisional artillery and ships offshore. The raid was costly in terms of casualties to the battalion – over 150, including twenty-seven dead – but it succeeded in preventing any German units moving to support their comrades facing the main Allied attack to the east.

On 1st (British) Division front, the Duke of Wellington's Regiment with a platoon of the Sherwood Foresters attached,

Casualties from 3rd Division near Cisterna.

attacked Pontoni and positions known as the 'King's Arms' and 'Green Bush Hill'. The assaults cost nearly 100 casualties, but they convinced the Germans that Pantoni could not be held and they abandoned it shortly afterwards. The division also mounted platoon-sized attacks on various points along the front, and contributed to the impression that the Via Anziate was to be used for the breakout by moving tanks along the Lateral Road.

General Truscott launched BUFFALO at 0545 hours on 23 May with a barrage delivered by over 1,000 weapons ranging from heavy artillery pieces to mortars and tank destroyers. At 0626 hours the barrage ceased and light bombers and fighter-bombers attacked the area around Cisterna; four minutes later the American divisions advanced.

By the evening 45th (US) Division had reached its objectives on the Cisterna-Campoleone railway line and had halted to consolidate and to await further developments to the east. Here 1st (US) Armored Division pushed its tanks forward to the railway line, and its infantry about 500 yards north of it, losing eleven tanks destroyed and forty-four damaged in the attack.

Cisterna Railway Bridge (left) and Station.

Further still to the right, on the line of the Mussolini Canal, First Special Service Force reached the railway north of Highway 7 by midday. It was counterattacked, unsuccessfully, during the afternoon, and was then relieved by two battalions from 34th (US) Division so that it might proceed with the following day's mission – to advance to Monte Arrestino.

The front held by *362nd Infantry Division* around Cisterna had been breached to a width of some two and one-half miles, and von Mackensen estimated that casualty rates were as high as fifty per cent. *715th Infantry Division* on the Mussolini Canal had had its front broken and had taken casualties of about sixty per cent, many of them inflicted by the artillery and air bombardments. Von Mackensen requested permission from Kesselring to disengage *LXXVI Panzer Corps* and to fall back on Sezze, but this was denied. Instead Kesselring ordered him to reform the front, reinforcing it with units from *I Parachute Corps*. Although he had reservations about weakening the west, where 1st and 5th (British) Divisions threatened to attack, von Mackensen moved the reconnaissance battalion across from *29 Panzer Grenadier Regiment* and warned *I Parachute Corps* to be prepared to follow it with units from *4th Parachute* and *65th Infantry Divisions*. To replace these units he called forward a regiment from *92nd Infantry Division* which was on coastal watch north of the River Tiber.

At 0530 hours on 24 May the Americans renewed their attack after thirty minutes of artillery preparation. 1st (US) Armored Division crossed Highway 7 by noon, and then Combat Command A pushed on towards Velletri while Combat Command B moved to the right and made for Colle Pautaleo. The drive to Velletri advanced no more than a mile through difficult ground against tenacious German anti-tank gunners. On the 3rd (US) Division front, 30 Infantry bypassed La Villa and reached Highway 7, leaving the town to be captured by the 1st Battalion of 7 Infantry Regiment. The Battalion then moved on to block Highway 7.

To the east of Cisterna 34th (US) Division continued its relief of First Special Service Force, and the 3rd Battalion of its 133 Infantry Regiment moved northwards along the Mussolini Canal to the Castellone area.

German response to the Allied advances was hindered by confusion and lack of information, as artillery and air barrages

German prisoner assisting with first aid on a 3rd Division soldier near Cisterna.

Tigers in Cisterna.

had done heavy damage to communications systems. It was possible to deduce, however, that as American troops were moving along the banks of the Mussolini Canal and as there were more of them to the northwest of Cisterna, that *954 Grenadier Regiment* from *362nd Infantry Division* was cut off in that town. Von Mackensen therefore authorised General Herr to withdraw *LXXVI Panzer Corps* to Sezze. He was ordered to hold a line running from Sezze to Colle Calvello via Priverno, and to make contact with *Tenth Army*; Herr was therefore to face VI Corps on one side, and II Corps, advancing from the east, on the other.

Combat Command A's advance on Velletri proceeded slowly on 25 May, still delayed by the German anti-tank gunners and by counterattacks. Combat Command B, supported by units from the divisional reserve, fared better and got to within a short distanced of Giulianello. In Cisterna, 7 Infantry Regiment had to engage in house-to-house fighting to clear *954 Grenadier Regiment* from the town. Having been cut off, the Germans elected to go down fighting, and drew the battle out until 1900 hours when the survivors surrendered.

Elsewhere, the Americans moved on Cori. 3rd Reconnaissance Troop and elements of 15 and 30 Infantry Regiments brushed aside resistance from the freshly arrived *1060 Grenadier Regiment* and the *Reconnaissance Battalion* of the *Hermann Göring Panzer Division*. The Germans, brought forward from the rear, had no time to familiarise themselves with the ground and were easily defeated. By nightfall First Special Service Force reached Monte Arrestino.

At 0731 hours on 25 May, east of the beachhead near Borgo Grappa, Brett Force from VI Corps (named after the commanding officer of 1st Reconnaissance Regiment who led it, and comprising 1st Battalion of 36 [US] Engineers, B Squadron of the Reconnaissance Regiment with some of their antitank guns, a battery of 25-pounders from 5th [British] Division, and a troop of American tank destroyers) met the 91st Cavalry Reconnaissance Squadron from 85th (US) Division. VI Corps and Fifth Army had linked up, 125 days after the initial Anzio landings. General Clark rushed to the scene to have the occasion preserved for posterity by the photographers.

Diversion to Rome

General Clark at Borgo Grappa. VI Corps and Fifth Army link.

General Truscott had achieved all of the first set of objectives of BUFFALO, and was about to move on Valmontone to complete the operation by blocking the German withdrawal. It was now, however, that Clark intervened by sending Brigadier General Brann to order him to divide his force and to block Highway 6 with 3rd (US) Division, the First Special Service Force and elements of 1st (US) Armored Division known as Howze Task Force, while the rest of VI Corps implemented Operation TURTLE as soon as possible – that is, to advance on the axis Carroceto-Campoleone-Rome.

Truscott was unhappy about this change of direction. In his memoirs he recorded his opinion that it had 'prevented the destruction of the German 10th Army', but his protests came to nothing. Brann stated that Clark was out of communication and that no discussion on the matter was therefore possible; Truscott

German prisoners.

accordingly prepared to execute TURTLE, dutiful if critical. He was aware that to do so would allow *Tenth Army* an escape route, but he had little choice in the matter. He ordered the operation to commence on 27 May, but Clark brought this date forward to noon on the day before. His rationale for the decision to divert towards Rome, to put the most charitable interpretation on it, was that as II (US) Corps had reached the Anzio beachhead he now had sufficient strength to both block Highway 6 and to capture Rome. The less charitable interpretation, supported by his own memoirs, was that he wanted the prize of taking the capital: 'Not only did we intend to become the first army in fifteen centuries to seize Rome from the south, but we intended to see that people back home knew that it was the Fifth Army that did the job and knew the price that had been paid for it.' That price was to include allowing the escape of much of *Tenth Army*, which would continue to fight and to inflict further casualties on the Allied armies.

Clark's desire to capture Rome deserves some discussion because of the implications of failing to block the German retreat. Clark had for some time harboured a resentment of the British, partly because of his and their part in the Salerno landings, which came very close to disaster. The Fifth Army, having made the landing, faced a well-prepared enemy who threatened to drive it back into the sea, a situation which it was able to retrieve without help from Montgomery's Eighth Army. However, the British press managed to portray the event so as to give Montgomery the credit for pulling the Americans' irons from the fire (an impression which was to be repeated on other occasions in northwest Europe, to the detriment of Anglo-American relations). To this was added Montgomery's rather tactless, and certainly patronising, attitude towards the American forces. Alexander's dealings directly with Truscott over the direction in which VI Corps was to head during the breakout from Anzio, in which he stated that BUFFALO was the only option, was yet another irritation to Clark, who saw it as by-passing him as Fifth Army commander. But inter-Allied competition apart, the overriding motivation for Clark's

German armour west of Campoleone Station.

decision to order Truscott to change direction was his craving for personal fame and glory. If he could achieve this before OVERLORD it would be a major coup – yet there was no likelihood of anyone else getting to Rome before the Fifth Army anyway: Alexander had made it clear from the outset that the city was in Clark's operational area, and it would be his for the taking when the moment was right.

The switch was more easily ordered than implemented, however. VI Corps had to halt, regroup, and form up to advance in a direction at ninety degrees to the original one. 1st (US) Armored Division had to fall back to the rear and then move across the 34th and 45th (US) Divisions to fresh assembly positions in the Padiglione Woods, which is where they had first concentrated after landing in January. Artillery and command posts and communications networks had to be reorganised and placed in new positions. In addition to this administrative problem, the new line of advance was to be along the Via Anziate, which is where the Germans had expected the breakout to occur and where they had assembled their strongest defences. On 26 May the redirected offensive was led by the 34th and 45th (US) Divisions, with the 36th Division on their right with Velletri as its objective.

To the left of the American force the two British divisions advanced northwest, and by nightfall on 28 May 1st (British) Division was in possession of Carroceto and the Factory, three months after it had last occupied it.

The heaviest fighting came when 45th (US) Division advanced to the northeast of Aprilia, and it became apparent that the attacks were not strong enough to break through the heavy German defences before Campoleone and Lanuvio. Truscott made the decision to commit 1st (US) Armored Division on 29 May, and by midday it cleared the last defenders from Campoleone Station. That afternoon Combat Command A advanced to the Albano road and then northwards, but the tanks soon outstripped their supporting infantry and they began to take casualties from German artillery and antitank guns. Twenty-one Shermans and sixteen M5 tank destroyers were knocked out. During the following day the Americans lost another twenty-three tanks and tank destroyers, without any compensating gain. TURTLE was failing: the Germans still held on firmly to Campoleone, Lanuvio and Velletri. 34th (US)

Division was having little success against the Caesar Line; having taken two strongpoints at San Gennaro and Villa Crocetta, the division was driven out by German counterattacks. To the division's left, the remainder of VI Corps' formations came to a halt, one after the other starting from the north and working south, as they ran into the German defences.

Any hope that Clark had of a swift advance to Rome through Albano and Highway 7 was rapidly eroding. The *3rd Panzer Grenadier, 65th Infantry* and parts of *4th Parachute Division*s effectively denied passage; their only withdrawals had been voluntary, to prepared positions on the Caesar Line. With its left flank firm on Velletri, *I Parachute Corps* swung its right wing back into the high ground of the Alban Hills. American attempts to dislodge it came to little; and their casualties for the period 23-30 May now amounted to 5,116, close to the numbers that the Germans had suffered during their attacks against the beachhead from 16 to 20 February. Mounting attacks directly at the strongest point of the Caesar Line was proving costly. Clark was going to have to think again.

The delay in reaching the Eternal City was beginning to worry Clark. To explain the change of VI Corps' advance he had told Alexander that enemy resistance had proved too strong for BUFFALO to reach its objective of sealing off Highway 7, and that implementing TURTLE would achieve the same aim by stopping *Tenth Army*'s withdrawal further west. This was

Between Cori and Valmontone. American vehicles waiting to advance.

patently untrue, and it did not take long for Alexander to realise it, although it was then too late to reverse Clark's action. On 25 and 26 May the German forces at Valmontone were not strong enough to stop VI Corps, but on 27 May Kesselring ordered *Tenth Army* to transfer some units to *LXXVI Corps* to bolster it, the *Hermann Göring Panzer Division* to attack and drive American forces back to new German defensive lines southeast of Velletri, and elements of *29th Panzer Grenadier Division* to join what was left of *715th Infantry Division*, all to create blocking positions which would stop VI Corps from reaching Highway 6 until *Tenth Army* had made its escape. The opportunity to close the trap decisively on the enemy had slipped from Clark's grasp.

Now Clark had to look for another route to Rome, and it appeared that the BUFFALO plan offered the solution, after all. But by now the German defences had firmed up and the opportunity of getting to the city this way would be more difficult to seize.

While the major part of VI Corps had been pushing down its dead-end road towards Rome, the First Special Service Force and 3rd (US) Division, with Howze Task Force attached, had moved on towards Artena on 26 May continuing with the mission to capture Valmontone and block Highway 6. 30 Infantry Regiment seized Rocca Massima that evening, and 15 Infantry Regiment prepared to take Artena the next day. It took up positions in the hills to the southwest of the town, while Howze Task Force moved to its west and made a reconnaissance almost as far as the highway. The cautious manner in which the advance was made served to give the Germans time to organise themselves, for they were poorly prepared to defend the Valmontone area at this time. *715th Infantry Division* was scattered following the earlier fighting, with the loss of all of its signals equipment and most of its heavy weapons; the reconnaissance battalion from the *Hermann Göring Panzer Division* had been pushed into Artena by the Americans, and *2 Hermann Göring Panzer Grenadier Regiment* was assembling near Labico. However, by the following day (27 May) when the Howze Task Force advanced towards Highway 6 it was driven back by artillery fire and withdrew to the railway line west of Artena. The town itself was captured by the Americans that afternoon, and then they took up defensive positions. A German counterattack was unsuccessful.

The American commander, General O'Daniel, felt that he was now in a position from which he could advance to cut Highway 6, but that the enemy facing him was too strong to take on with the limited forces at his disposal – had the whole of VI Corps been where it should have been under the BUFFALO plan, there would have been no such problem. Apart from other considerations, to move forward would have been to expose his right flank, a situation which would not be resolved until II (US) Corps and the French Expeditionary Corps arrived from the east on 29 May.

On 30 May General Truscott gave consideration to the problem of the stalemate at Lanuvio. The possibility of using 36th (US) Division to flank the position from the east by pushing into the Alban Hills, while 34th (US) Division carried out the same manoeuvre to the west, was being mooted when General Walker, the commander of 36th Division, reported that his patrols had discovered a very thinly-held portion of the German line on the Velletri-Valmontone road. Monte Artemisio, to its west, appeared to be unoccupied and there was a usable track running up it. Capture of the mountain would give a commanding site over the Alban Hills from which operations

Anzio Annie captured in Civatavecchia.

could be mounted in any direction. Truscott ordered Walker to seize the mountain that night.

The reason for the skimpy German defence in front of Monte Artemisio was that it was here that the *Hermann Göring Panzer* and *362nd Infantry Divisions'* (from I *Parachute Corps* and *LXXVI Panzer Corps* respectively) boundaries met; but they had failed to interlock. The Germans had realised that the mountain was undefended, and General Herr had ordered that troops be sent there; but before they could get into position the Americans had acted and the opportunity was lost.

36th (US) Division mounted a holding attack on Velletri with 141 Regiment while 142 and 143 Regiments silently penetrated the German lines, one after the other, and pushed on to the mountain crest. 142 Regiment then moved southwest to the Maschio dell' Artemisio, two miles northwest of Velletri, while 143 went north to capture the Maschio d'Ariano and Point 931 which overlooked the Valmontone gap. 143 Regiment began to establish observation points on the summit of their mountain, from which there were commanding views in an arc from the east to the south west. The targets were plentiful, so many in fact that the forward observers had trouble in dealing with all of them and finding sufficient batteries to bring fire down. As a priority they attended to the road to Velletri to keep the Germans the garrison isolated. Both Velletri and Valmontone fell to the Allies on 2 June.

General Lemelsen.

Recriminations on the German side were not long in coming. Von Mackensen had belatedly attempted to deal with the hole in the front line between I *Parachute Corps* and *LXXVI Panzer Corps*, but an assault by the only available battalion got nowhere. He offered his resignation before Kesselring could sack him, an offer which was accepted. General Lemelsen took his place as commander of the *Fourteenth Army*. Once the Allies had captured the Valmontone gap German resistance fell apart and *I Parachute Corps* and *LXXVI Panzer Corps* fell back towards Tivoli. Kesselring requested, and obtained, permission from Hitler to withdraw from Rome without making a last-ditch stand, and on 3 June the German rearguard left the Alban Hills.

The following morning, 4 June, the first Americans entered Rome. From which unit they came is uncertain – the rush to win the prize of being first led many to enter the race, and amongst the claimants are First Special Service Force and 88th (US) Infantry Division – but by midnight the centre of the Eternal City and half of the strategic Tiber bridges were controlled by Fifth Army. On the northern roads to the city some German rearguards still blocked the way during the afternoon, holding off the First Special Service Force. Their presence, within the city limits, meant that Clark could not yet say that he had taken Rome. He demanded, and got, the Germans cleared out of the city in time to have his photograph taken beside a city sign – 'Roma' – for the press, that same day. The sign was later removed and taken to the United States as a personal souvenir.

Clark had achieved his quest for glory, but it was to be short-lived. The fall of Rome on 4 June was eclipsed in the world's press by the Normandy landings, OVERLORD, on 6 June 1944.

Afternote

SHINGLE was an operation which has generated a great deal of debate, both amongst the participants and historians. While it is not the purpose of this book to argue the issues in depth, it would nevertheless be wrong not to mention them in outline. Were the Anzio-Nettuno landings a mistake, and – under different leadership – could they ever have been decisive in the Italian campaign?

The whole concept of landing a single corps so far behind enemy lines with the objective of cutting their lines of communication appears attractive until it is examined more closely. A number of individuals criticised the idea at the time of its planning and execution, amongst them General Lucas, the man tasked with carrying out the mission. As described earlier, Lucas felt that to move his command inland to capture the Alban Hills would be to risk its annihilation; it would be cut off from its base. Clark gave him some support in this view, and it was not without foundation. Alexander and Churchill, who

The captured German gun, Anzio Annie, provides a setting for a photograph of American nurses.

argued forcefully for the operation, felt differently – but that does not make them right. Another consideration is whether VI Corps would have been strong enough, even had the problem of safeguarding its logistic link to the sea been resolved, to block enough German routes to seriously threaten the viability of the Gustav Line. Highways 6 and 7 ran north and south of the Alban Hills respectively; one might have been blocked effectively, but two may have proved too ambitious. The other concern is the length of time Lucas would have had to hold out before Fifth Army broke through and reached him.

On the positive side, however, the presence of VI Corps stretched the German front from eighty-five miles on 21 January to 120 miles at the end of the month. Kesselring had no option but to address this threat by containing the Anzio beachhead, thereby meeting Alexander's objective of tying down German divisions which might otherwise have been sent to face the

Lieutenant General Sir Oliver W. H. Leese, Bt., K.C.B., C.B.E., D.S.O. He took over command of the 8th Army in Italy, January 1944.

Allied forces land at Anzio. X-RAY Yellow Beach.

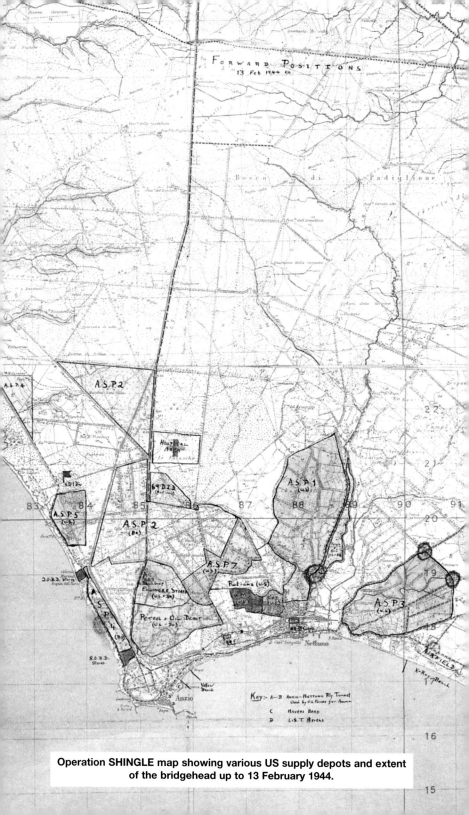

Operation SHINGLE map showing various US supply depots and extent of the bridgehead up to 13 February 1944.

Mines were a constant hazard, particularly during the landings, when the Allies suffered casualties as they pushed inland from the beaches. Particularly dangerous were the wooden-cased anti-personnel mines (bottom right) which could not be detected by the magnetic mine-detectors, and which had to be cleared by hand.

Anzio harbour.
German infantry counter-attack.

Victorious German infantry contain the bridgehead.

German propaganda leaflet. 'The road to Rome is...'

PAVED WITH SKULLS!

American Rangers captured at Anzio are marched through the Piazza Venezia. Inset: a German cartoon had the British saying 'My God! I'd like to have a word or two with the character who coined "All roads lead to Rome".' An Allied victory parade through Piazza Venezia two months later.

This battle-weary column of American GIs march north in pursuit of the withdrawing Germans.

Commander of the US Fifth Army, General Mark Clark, and his chief of staff, General Gruenther, arrive at Vatican City the day after their entry into Rome.

OVERLORD landings. At the level of global strategy, therefore, SHINGLE may be judged to have achieved its purpose; at the theatre level, the Germans around Anzio could not be used to reinforce the Gustav Line, even if they were not sent to France.

Underlying the whole issue, however, was the lack of a fully agreed and co-ordinated strategy between the Allies for the Italian campaign. As explained earlier, Britain and America (or at least those tasked with promulgating the war in Europe) had different hopes and expectations for Italy. The American attitude was somewhat lukewarm, and their insistence on diverting resources to the forthcoming invasion of Normandy – both men and materiel – could not but detract from the odds for success of an operation such as the Anzio landings. With these limitations, it is arguable that SHINGLE should never have been mounted in the first place. Without sufficient force on the beachhead, and the ability to support it, the operation was always going to carry an element of risk – but so does every operation in war.

As to the question of whether or not a general other than Lucas would have made a difference, the answer must surely be

Citizens of Rome greet the allies.

in the negative, for it was less a matter of leadership than that the plan itself was flawed. If the force that landed on 22 January was not strong enough to achieve the aim of capturing the

Alban Hills, then whoever commanded it would have failed. Another general may have chosen to take the risk of advancing swiftly inland, but the odds are that sooner or later he would have lost his corps. What effect he might have had before he did so, is a matter for conjecture.

In other respects, Lucas did not show himself to be particularly good at commanding a bi-national force. He readily admitted that he did not understand the British, and he seems to have made little effort to remedy the situation; indeed, not only did he not get out onto the ground to familiarise himself with his ally's condition, he failed to do so with units of his own nation's army. The situation improved immeasurably when Truscott took over. Not only was he a more 'hands-on' general, he had served with the British

General Lucas was relieved of his command when he failed to drive inland.

before, and there was a mutual respect between him and the soldiers of that nation which eased many potential problems.

At the lower levels of command, inter-Allied relations appear to have been very good from the outset. At times British and American units were interspersed with each other, fighting shoulder to shoulder, rather than having clearly defined areas of the front line demarcated along national lines. During the fighting in early February, for instance, 24 Guards Brigade had 3/504th US Parachute Infantry under command; the Irish Guards' regimental history speaks warmly of the close relationship between the commanding officers of the respective units. American parachute companies were employed to plug gaps in the British line whenever they occurred.

The next question, which has caused somewhat less debate, is Clark's decision to switch from the BUFFALO to the TURTLE plan. The opinions here are more in agreement, despite Clark's self-justification for taking the course of action that he did. The body of opinion at the time was against him, with Alexander and Truscott amongst those who condemned Clark for choosing self-glory over closing the Valmontone gap to prevent sizable amounts of the German *Tenth Army* to escape. However, it must

Rome – liberated.

German 'human torpedos' attempted an attack on the Anzio anchorage on the night of 20 April. The craft consisted of two standard 21-inch torpedos fastened together, one complete with warhead (slung underneath), the other, the control torpedo has a cockpit in place of the warhead. These photographs are of the control torpedo. The operator's circular hatch can be seen in the upper and bottom left photographs; it was covered by dome of glass or transparent plastic. When the position was suitable for an attack the armed torpedo was started up and released whereupon it proceeded under its own propulsion to the target. The operator then attempted to circle about and return to his parent ship. The torpedo shown in these pictures beached three miles north of Anzio. The operator was unable to extricate himself and had to be helped out by Allied troops.

be accepted that Clark's view that Valmontone was not the only route that the Germans could take westwards is valid. The Eighth Army advance up the Liri valley was not well handled, and its slowness, caused by the congestion as division after division tried to cram forward up narrow roads, did much to ease the Germans' withdrawal. Regardless of Alexander's plan to block their escape at Valmontone, there were other routes that they could, and did, take. There was little Allied effort to operate north of the Liri, for example, which allowed the German left wing to retire relatively unhampered. Alexander has been criticised for his fixation on concentrating Eighth Army along Highway 6 instead of also using the hills north and south of it. In the event, the French were able to push through the mountains and could have been used to better effect to seal off *Tenth Army*'s withdrawal. This does not, however, excuse Clark's action. He was not to know that Eighth Army's progress would be as slow as it was, his failure to reach Valmontone at the earliest opportunity undoubtedly allowed large numbers of Germans to escape (regardless of those on other routes), and he deliberately ignored his superior officer's intentions.

Whatever the views of the above issues, some facts are not disputed. Some 7,000 Allies and an estimated 5,000 Germans died in the fighting in and around the beachhead during the months of January to June 1944. At the time of writing (the figures change as bodies are still being found), 3,371 British and Commonwealth sailors, soldiers and airmen from the battles around Anzio are buried in the two CWGC Cemeteries in Anzio; the names of the missing are inscribed on the memorial tablets at Cassino. While the British and Commonwealth tradition has been to establish large numbers of comparatively small cemeteries close to each battlefield, other nations have their own conventions. For the Americans, the graves of some of the dead from the fighting around Anzio, and the names of the missing are to be found at the American Cemetery in Nettuno, together with those who died in campaigns from Sicily and throughout Italy. Not all of those who fell around Anzio are buried here, for some bodies were repatriated to the United States. 27,443 German casualties are buried, together with those who fell in the areas around Rome, in the German Cemetery in Pomezia.

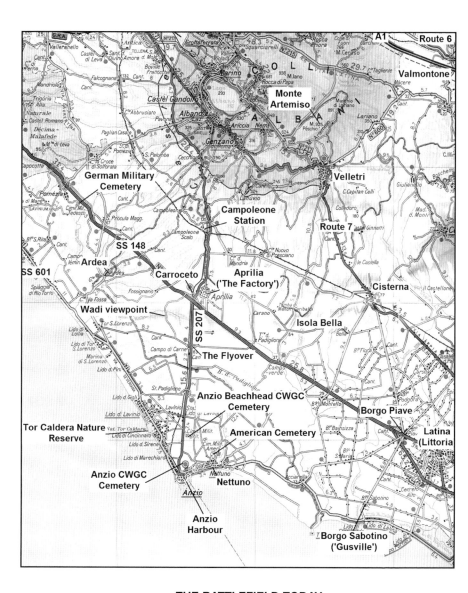

THE BATTLEFIELD TODAY

A significant problem in visiting key sites on the battlefield is that much of the ground has been changed through building and agricultural development, and large-scale maps of the area are hard to come by. Some of the principal locations mentioned in the text are highlighted on a modern map of the area. This, together with the directions given in each chapter, should enable readers to find their way to the sites described.

Chapter One

THE COASTAL STRIP

PETER Beach

The three landing beaches are only partly accessible today. The westernmost of them, PETER Beach (the British landing) may be overlooked from the Tor Caldera Regional Nature Reserve, which is open on selected days each week, less often during the winter months. Nevertheless, it is worth making the visit to walk through the park to the Tower, from which a clear view is obtained westwards along the beach. The park grounds also contain the remnants of British trenches, which have a brief description of the battle displayed alongside them. They are well signposted and easily found.

PETER Beach. Shermans with wading gear come ashore under the protection of a Bofors anti-aircraft crew.

103

LSTs unloading on PETER Beach.

From the tower, which is 2,000 yards east of PETER Beach, the difficulties experienced during the landings can be readily understood. The routes inland have to find their way through the cliffs and sand dunes, and the thick undergrowth presented a barrier to vehicle movement. What is less obvious is the sandbank which lay under the surface of the water in 1944, and which prevented the deeper-draught vessels from reaching the shoreline.

The Landing

Beach reconnaissance

From late November 1943 onwards the reconnaissance of PETER Beach was carried out by folboat (two-man collapsible canoes) teams from a Combined Operations Pilotage Party and from Z Special Boat Section. These operations were intended to establish the beach conditions for landing personnel and vehicles, and to discover the extent of enemy defences of the area. They were very hazardous and not without mishap or casualties.

During the night of 2-3 December, for example, three folboats were launched from *Moto Silurante 24*, an Italian Navy vessel now under command of the Royal Navy, off the intended landing beach. The mission, codenamed Operation PWQ, was led by Sub-Lieutenant KG Patterson RANVR, with AB GD Lockhead as his number two in the canoe. The two other folboats were manned by Captain WG Davis and CSM

Commando at Anzio slung with a Mk 2 Bren gun.

Galloway and Captain AR McClair and Sergeant R Sidlow, all from the SBS.

At 0045 hours on 3 December *MS 24* made landfall fifty yards northeast of Torre Caldara and the canoeists set off on their missions. Captain Davis headed for the shore, while Captain McClair paddled northwest to find the beach he had been tasked with investigating. After three-quarters of a mile he met Sub-Lieutenant Patterson, and informed him that it was his belief that they were out of position. While they were talking, their folboats were almost swamped by a large wave; the sea and the wind were rising, and visibility deteriorating. Patterson turned towards the shore to clarify his position, which was the last that was seen of him and Lockhead.

McClair continued on course and swam ashore at about 0200 hours to get the required information. By now the wind and sea had risen, and visibility had deteriorated. After twenty minutes he set course to return to the parent vessel, and was aboard it by 0320 hours.

Meanwhile Capt Davis and CSM Galloway, whose task it was to reconnoitre the southern extremity of PETER Beach near

Sketch from Major Davis' report on Operation PWQ

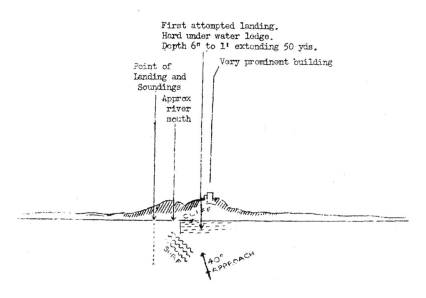

SILHOUETTE OF COAST AT TORRE CALDARA

First attempted landing.
Hard under water ledge.
Depth 6" to 1' extending 50 yds.

Very prominent building

Point of
Landing and
Soundings

Approx
river
mouth

40° APPROACH

Torre Caldara, made soundings of the water depth offshore, and returned to MS 24 at 0225 hours, having seen lights flashing about half a mile further down the coast.

Nothing more was heard of Sub-Lieutenant Patterson and AB Lockhead, and the assumption was that their folboat had foundered in the surf. Although both McClair and Sidlow thought that they had heard voices from the shore, neither was certain enough to suggest turning back, and the two sailors had to be reported missing, presumed killed.

This incident was not the only one in which casualties happened off PETER Beach. During the early hours of 30 December, US Navy Ensigns KE Howe and M Pirro failed to return to their parent vessel, PT Boat 201. Captain Davis, commanding the party, considered that the Americans had either overturned their folboat or could not find their way back; with the calm sea, the latter alternative seemed more likely. Two other crews (Captain Davis and CSM Galloway, both RA; and Sub-Lieutenant T Williams RNVR and Ensign J G Donnell USN) returned safely.

Shortly after midnight on 22 January, Allied Task Force Peter dropped anchor offshore, having been guided into place by marker submarines, that for Peter Beach being HMS *Ultor*. The final approaches were signed by folboat crews from the Combined Operations Pilotage Parties, flashing marker lights out to sea. The landing craft were lowered and loaded with troops from the transports, the LSIs *Sobieska*, *Glengyle* and *Derbyshire*, and formed up into their assault formations, and at 0100 hours the LCT(R)s off each beach opened fire with their barrage of missiles beyond and to either side of the landing areas. They elicited no response from the shore, not even from the machinegun posts which aerial reconnaissance had shown to be established near the Tor Caldera. The first waves of troops, from 2nd Battalion of the North Staffordshire Regiment and 6th Battalion, The Gordon Highlanders disembarked from their assault boats ten minutes later, but – their vessels having grounded on the sandbank – had to wade the last hundred yards to firm ground.

Apart from sparsely laid mines of wooden construction which made detection by magnetic means impossible, there was no sign of enemy preparation to resist the landing. Six men were killed and another fourteen wounded before a path was cleared through the mines. The two battalions moved inland through the undergrowth to the coastal road. An hour later, the time it took for the assault craft to complete the round trip back to the transports and return to the beach, the second waves of infantry, comprising 1st Battalion, The Loyal Regiment and 1st Battalion, The Scots Guards, arrived. They moved westwards and eastwards along the coast, respectively, to secure the beachhead. The only enemy encountered were a few Germans convalescing in a beach hut, and still in their pyjamas.

At dawn, the scene was one of industrious, but peaceful, activity. Numerous vessels of all sizes worked back and forth under the shelter of barrage balloons, protected by antiaircraft guns which as yet had no job to do. On the beaches vehicles had to be winched up the slopes of the sand dunes before moving inland. The Grenadier and Irish Guards, the remainder of 24 Guards Brigade, landed at 0700 hours, being ferried from their LCIs on the sandbank to the shore by a fleet of DUKWs. Major Young, of the Irish Guards, bore a large umbrella on his arm, and – according to the regimental history – 'stepped ashore with the air of a missionary visiting a South Sea island and surprised to see no cannibals'. The umbrella was not merely an affectation, for it provide shelter from rain when raised over a slit-trench and indicated the owner's position to his men.

Cannibals there were not to be, nor Germans either. The two brigades pushed inland, but only as far as the Padiglione Woods. Much of the day was spent in inactivity, while the soldiers on the ground wondered whether or not an opportunity was being lost. Churchill would have agreed that it was. That night was an extremely cold one, which the troops weathered without benefit of greatcoats, blankets or tents, having nothing more than what they had brought ashore with them. 23 January was, for them, another wasted day, with nothing happening except the unloading of vehicles joining the units from Anzio harbour, and some rather vague preparations to deal with any counterattack. Meanwhile, of course, the German headquarters was a hive of activity as Kesselring put together his plans to deal with the landings.

Anzio

Drive eastwards down the coast to Anzio on the SS601. Take the **right turn** onto the road towards the harbour, just past the lighthouse. The road follows the beach down to the harbour, but shortly before reaching it, on the left is the statue of 'Angelita of Anzio', which represents one of the strangest stories of the time.

In 1961 the mayor of Anzio was contacted by a British veteran of the conflict, who wrote that his unit had 'adopted' a five-year old girl who they had found abandoned at the time of the landings. She was identified as Angelita Rossi, from a label in her clothing, who had been on holiday in the area. Her family could not be found, and so she stayed with the unit for several days, with the permission of the platoon commander, until she was killed by enemy shellfire. The veteran, Corporal Christopher Hayes of the Royal Scots Fusiliers, was hoping that the girl's parents had been traced, a task which he and his comrades had determined to achieve. They were unable to do so because only the platoon commander (who had since died) and Hayes himself were the sole survivors of the battle; indeed, his whole company had been wiped out. The Italian press took up the story, which attracted national interest. In Britain, Hayes was interviewed and his story told in a magazine article; but it now differed in detail from the original.

Did five-year old Angelita die in the arms of Corporal Haynes?

In 1965 an Italian woman came forward, claiming to be Angelita, and recounted a story of surviving her wounds. The Italians arranged for Hayes to come to Anzio to meet her, but on

X-RAY Yellow Beach. The casino is the building with the two cupolas.

Memorial plaque to the Rangers, on the wall of the old casino.

arrival in the town he angrily repudiated her claim. Angelita, he stated, had died in his arms from a fatal head wound – the Italian woman was no more than a pretender (one of several) who sought to benefit from being identified as the child. Hayes also accused the Anzio authorities of encouraging the woman's story to boost tourist publicity for the town. As far as Hayes was concerned, the headline-seeking Italians were attempting to cash in from the touching story of a dead child, which had meant so much to him.

The story did not stop there, however, for interested journalists kept the investigation going. They began to question Hayes' story, which began to look doubtful once the details were examined. For example, he had claimed that most of his platoon had been killed in January and February 1944, whereas those members of his battalion who were interred in the local cemeteries did not die until March at the earliest. This was unsurprising – 2nd Battalion The Royal Scots Fusiliers did not arrive in the beachhead until 7 March. Hayes had also claimed that his platoon commander had since died, but he proved to be very much still alive. Nor did the story that Angelita was in the area on holiday in January 1944 seem credible, although language difficulties might excuse confusion on this point, especially when trying to communicate with a terrified five-year old. The inconsistencies in the story remain unresolved, and are likely to remain so. What ever the truth of the matter, the statue was erected as a symbol of the innocent victims of

X-RAY Beach.

American engineers checking for mines on Anzio beach.

GIs waiting along the sea wall.

war – the children who were, and are, caught up in it, often with fatal consequences.

Continue into the harbour.

On the wall to the right of the road when entering the harbour are memorial plaques commemorating events and units involved in the Anzio battles. The 1st Battalion Duke of Wellington's Regiment landed here as part of 1st (British) Division on 23 January. As their LCI edged into the harbour – they had been diverted here from the difficult PETER Beach – the soldiers witnessed an LCT, which was landing vehicles onto the quay, hit by enemy shellfire. The lessons of the event did not go unheeded, for as soon as the two gangplanks were run out the battalion doubled ashore at speed, before moving inland through the busy streets to take up their positions north of Anzio.

There is also a memorial to those crewmembers of HMS *Spartan* who died when the cruiser was sunk off Nettuno

LSTs in Anzio Harbour.

HMS *Spartan*, sunk by German aircraft off Nettuno.

on 29 January. The ship had been providing anti-aircraft cover for vessels in the harbour and off the beaches when enemy aircraft attacked at 1750 hours, approaching the Allied shipping from the east so as to silhouette them against the afterglow of the setting sun. They released a number of glider bombs, one of which struck the cruiser behind 'B' funnel, starting a fire and causing flooding below decks. At 1915 hours she sank. Five officers and forty-one ratings were posted killed or missing presumed killed, and a further forty-two ratings were wounded.

The harbour itself was the objective of the 1st and 4th Ranger battalions on 22 January. As described earlier, they landed on X-RAY Yellow Beach, and took the harbour with little resistance from the German unit which was supposed to have destroyed it. Yellow Beach lies below the casino (which can be identified by the two white cupolas on the roof) further along the bay to the north of the harbour itself. There is a Ranger memorial on the casino wall, which gives a brief outline of the part the three battalions played in the fighting in January 1944. On 22 January, the beach was potentially the most hazardous one on which to land, for the sea wall had a belt of barbed wire surmounting it, behind which were sturdy buildings which could easily have been turned into strongpoints from which to cover any landing with fire. Indeed, further along the beach to the east was a pillbox, which since the war years has been transformed into a sculpture, but which offered no resistance in 1944.

The Rangers, supported by engineers whose task it was to clear away any prepared demolitions, found no enemy resistance until they reached the railway bridge to the north of town. Here German machine-gunners killed one Ranger before being overcome. By 0300 hours the men of the 3rd Rangers had passed through the first two battalions and were on their way to capture a German battery north of the town. This they did without incident, the gunners having prudently withdrawn. Apart from a brief brush with German armoured cars in Anzio, the town was in Allied hands and the harbour facilities undamaged. Links were swiftly made with 2 Special Service Brigade, which occupied the higher ground north of Anzio between 2 (British) Infantry Brigade on PETER Beach to the west and the town itself.

X-RAY Red and Green Beaches are further down the coast, now within the grounds of the Italian Army artillery range which lies to the east of Nettuno, and are not normally accessible to the public – not that there is much to see there today, time and post-war development having wrought their changes. It makes sense, for the sake of uniformity, to deal with the events there on 22 January here. Some of the landing beach to the east of Nettuno can be seen from the Anzio mole.

The X-RAY landing by 3rd (US) Division went, according to Truscott, 'Like clockwork'. The troops landed on time and in the right place, and the only obstacle offered by the enemy was a minefield at one end of the beach, which was obligingly well marked. A few Germans were captured, some still abed, and the Americans were able to push inland without hindrance. This beach did not suffer from the problems experienced at PETER, of sandbanks offshore and difficult sand dunes on the coast, and the Americans were soon at the initial Beach Defence Line. Patrols started to capture the bridges over the Mussolini Canal.

Anzio harbour – the buildup

The harbour of Anzio, small though it is, was the only place that the larger craft could dock to disembark men and materiel, and its capture was essential to the success of the operation. Even after being taken, virtually intact, on the first day, its use was thereafter subject to enemy artillery and aerial bombardment right up until the breakout from the beachhead in May. Contemporary photographs show the state of the harbourside buildings during the battles, which were regularly hit by fire from the Alban Hills. In the harbour itself, LSTs packed the seafront, disembarking lorries full of materiel which drove straight to the supply dumps, before re-embarking lorries and ambulances containing casualties for the return trip to Naples. DUKWs ferried supplies from transports offshore to the beaches where the Rangers had landed on D Day, and to X-RAY Beach.

The problems of the time spent unloading LSTs when under fire in the harbour led to an innovation which has since become commonplace: the roll-on, roll-off procedure whereby fully loaded vehicles were driven off the LSTs and straight to the supply dumps, to be immediately replaced on the ships by empty trucks, or those carrying wounded personnel or other loads returning to Naples. The reduction in time spent by the ships under fire was considerable, and led to both lives and equipment being saved.

Seventy percent of the American Quartermaster Corps in the Anzio beachhead were coloured troops. Their role included unloading ships in Anzio harbour and driving the supplies to the various dumps which they maintained ashore: ammunition, rations, fuel, medical supplies, and so on. During the first week of the landing 500 men of the 387th Engineer Battalion, a coloured unit, manhandled an average of 1,940 tons of supplies ashore daily.

These areas suffered regular bombing raids and shellfire, and casualties were taken among the personnel here. It was felt necessary to rotate logistic units out of the combat zone for a period of rest every six weeks, to Sorrento or some other location away from the conflict, a luxury that not all servicemen experienced during their time at Anzio.

The Anzio Beachhead Museum *(Museo dello Sbarco di Anzio)* and the Archaeological Museum are located in the Villa Adele, on Via di Villa Adele, just downhill from the town's railway station. The beachhead museum contains a collection of uniforms, equipment and photographs from the battles.

Nettuno
Drive into Nettuno past the Forte Sangallo on the sea front. The citadel contains a small but interesting museum in which are displayed articles from the landings, situated in the rooms that,

in 1944, were occupied by the Office of Strategic Services.

One of the concerns of the OSS was psychological warfare, which both sides employed during the Italian campaign. Allied troops in the beachhead were subjected to German leafleting, with pamphlets designed to lower morale delivered by artillery and mortar shells. Pamphlets drew parallels with Dunkirk, with the promise that the 1940 experience of British evacuation was about to be repeated here. 'Beachhead-Death's Head' proclaimed some; others depicted a British wife or girl-friend back at home pulling on her stockings beside a dishevelled bed, while a smug-looking American was getting dressed behind her. The message, and the intent, was obvious. Propaganda aimed at the Americans was framed in a different manner, contrasting the profiteers back in the States to the 'dough-boys' who were risking life and limb on the front line. Other outputs described the Anzio beachhead as being an enormous prisoner of war camp, which even excused the Germans the problem of feeding the inmates. Little, if any, of these attempts had success, although instructions on how to feign illness in order to be evacuated to a rear hospital, which were printed on the back of matchboxes, may have been more effectual. There were a

German propaganda leaflets.

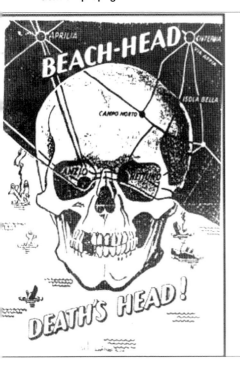

THE BEACH-HEAD

is going to be the big blow against the Germans.

Wasn't that the slogan of three months ago ?

TODAY

It is still a beach-head and nothing else.

But it is now paved with the skulls of thousands of British and American soldiers !

The Beach - Head has become a Death's Head!

It is welcoming You with a grin, and also those who are coming after you across the sea for an appointment with death.

Do they know what they are in for? Yes, they feel that they are landing on a

DEATH'S HEAD

'Axis Sally' (Mildred Gillars) – a 'mug-shot' after her arrest.

number of Allied soldiers who sought a way out of the unceasing grind and stress of life at Anzio, and self-inflicted wounds were not unknown.

Another propaganda tool used by the Germans was the broadcasts of 'Axis Sally', who reported Allied misfortunes with relish, in a sultry, sexy voice. With a male colleague named George, Sally would play jazz music interspersed with messages which highlighted Allied personalities: giving the names of prisoners of war, for example. They also repeated the mantra, 'Go easy boys. There's danger ahead,' which became repeated by American troops; just what the Germans had intended. Sally was not all that she sounded, however. An American, whose real name was Mildred Gillars, she had married a German before the war, and began broadcasting propaganda for Radio Berlin. Her real-life appearance did not live up to the image that she projected on air, and her affect on the morale of troops in Italy seems to have been somewhat less than she, and the Germans, had hoped for.

Continue down the road to the Piazza Mazzini, where it may be possible to park.

On the surrender of the Italians on 9 September 1943, the Germans occupied the towns of Anzio and Nettuno to disarm their now untrustworthy former ally. They moved an anti-tank gun to the front of the Italian garrison building in the Piazza Mazzini in Nettuno, the large pink house on the western side of the Piazza, and fired into the first floor. The opening of hostilities generated a revolt among the civilian population, and a number of them, led by Angelo Lauri, an Italian tank corps second lieutenant, armed themselves with rifles, submachine guns, grenades and an unreliable heavy machinegun before barricading themselves into the Forte Sangallo and the Belvedere. Having rendered all but one of the tanks at the firing range inoperable, Lauri drove it into the Piazza Mazzini. He was joined by a small unit of infantry from Fogliano, and some who had escaped from the Piave Barracks, which were in the town to the north, where the Italian commander had surrendered to the Germans. Some troops ignored the order and turned on the Germans, who retreated down the Via Santa Barbara only to come under fire from the Italians in the Forte Sangallo.

The Germans were driven out of the town, but did not waste time before returning in greater strength. Elements of the *Hermann Göring Division*, en route for Cassino, were diverted to Anzio and then Nettuno, supported by a Stuka attack. On the 12 September a cease-fire was arranged and the Italians surrendered. Reprisals were swift in coming: firing squads carried out executions against the walls of the Piazza Mazzini - the bullet scars are still evident. One of those summarily executed was a boy who had been found in possession of a pair of pliers shortly after the Germans' telephone wires had been cut, shot in front of a group of women waiting for travel permits. Much of the area was evacuated by order of the Germans. Locals were forbidden to be closer than five kilometres from the coast on pain of death, apart from those employed by the Germans as bakers and cleaners – or more ominously – in laying minefields. Of the population of about

Bullet scars on the walls of the Piazza Mazzini.

Headquarters VI Corps today.

G4 Branch in VI Corps Headquarters beneath the streets.

12,000 only a handful remained, the rest being forced to move inland.

After the war a marble plaque was erected in the Piazza Mazzini in remembrance of the rising. The inscription on it reads 'In questa piazza ad iniziativa di alcuni animosi il popolo di Nettuno insorse contro i nazi-fascisti. 8-9-10 settembre 1943' ('In this square, on the initiative of a number of brave-spirited citizens, the people of Nettuno rose against the Nazi-fascists on 8-9-10 September 1943') The dates are incorrect, however; the rising started on the 9 September.

On the north side of the Piazza is the Via Romana, and a few steps away on the corner of the Vicolo Cieco, a small pedestrian thoroughfare, is a shop on which a plaque indicates that it was in the cellars of this house that General Lucas established his VI Corps Headquarters. A little further along the street, in a small precinct to the right, the Piazza del Mercato, is another plaque on the house in which Generals Lucas and Truscott lived during the campaign. Beneath the houses American engineers had opened up the cellars so that they interconnected and were able to contain the offices of the various staff branches.

The area in and around Nettuno, including the artillery ranges, contained the American hospitals and an airstrip for light aircraft.

The Medical Services
Medical planning for SHINGLE made full use of the experience gained in Africa, Sicily and Salerno. Each of the formations making up VI (US) Corps had its organic medical units – the Regimental Aid Posts, Field Dressing Stations, and so on. In addition, the American 52nd Medical Battalion, 93rd, 95th, and 56th Evacuation Hospitals and the 33rd Field Hospital (which had the British 12th Field Transfusion Unit attached); and the British 2nd Casualty Clearing Station, the 549th Ambulance Company, and a detachment of the 2nd Auxiliary Surgical Group, were to support the landing. Working on the assumption that ten per cent of the assault troops and five per cent of the remainder would become casualties on D Day, and that thereafter there would be five hospital cases per 1,000 men daily, it was considered that these medical resources would be adequate.

For the landing itself, aid stations were to land with the first

121

US Hospital after bombardment.
An American nurse digging in.

troops. On the American beach, the 52nd Medical Battalion was to set up a casualty collecting and clearing station to evacuate wounded personnel to hospital ships. 33rd Field Hospital was to deal with those who could not be moved. The 93rd and 95th Evacuation Hospitals, each of which had 400 beds, were also to land on D Day. On the British beach, two Field Dressing Stations and a Beach Dressing Station, supported by 2nd Casualty Clearing Station were to provide medical cover. Offshore, hospital ships were to be available until D+3, after which time they were on-call to the senior medical officer ashore.

As recounted earlier, casualties during the landings were minimal, which meant that the landing plans could be amended to give priority to combatants and their materiel. The relatively few casualties were evacuated onto LSTs or cared for at the battalion aid stations and Regimental Aid Posts, and the only non-organic medical facility to establish itself ashore on D Day was 2nd Platoon from the 33rd Field Hospital, which set up its hospital on the beach south east of Nettuno and was ready to receive patients from about 1800 hours. For two days this was the only beachhead hospital, utilising three operating tables continuously. A backlog of some twenty to thirty cases soon built up as the fighting inland increased, and the hospital came under shellfire, although without sustaining casualties. The other platoons from the Field Hospital came ashore on D+1, and their personnel were used to augment those of 2nd Platoon.

The 93rd and 95th Evacuation Hospitals landed on 23 January, and came into operation the following day, the first in Anzio itself, the second between Anzio and Nettuno. The British 2nd Casualty Clearing Station opened to the north of Anzio at the same time, near to the site of the present Beach Head Commonwealth War Graves Cemetery.

Three British Hospital Ships, HMHS *St. David*, HMHS *St. Andrew*, and HMHS *Leinster* were offshore. Despite being clearly marked with red crosses and well-illuminated, they came under attack from the Luftwaffe during the night of 24 January. HMHS *St David*, which had 226 patients and medical staff aboard, received a direct hit and sank. The 130 survivors were rescued by HMS *Leinster*, which had also been damaged. One of those who died was Captain Jenkin Robert Oswald Thompson RAMC. Having organised parties to evacuate the wounded from the sinking vessel, he went below decks to comfort the last casualty, who was trapped. For this action, he was awarded a posthumous George Cross. Captain Thompson had previously been cited for bravery aboard hospital ships at Dunkirk and Salerno. He is commemorated on the Brookwood Memorial in England.

The hospitals, in the confined beachhead, constantly came under enemy artillery and air attack. Frequent shelling and air raids made evacuation of casualties from the beaches hazardous, and the waiting ships were an easy target, as evidenced by the fate of *St David*. As the German resistance strengthened, these attacks became more frequent, particularly with the arrival of the long-range railway guns on the Alban Hills. The hospitals were at times no more than six miles behind the front lines.

As it became obvious that the hospitals were extremely vulnerable to enemy action it was decided to move them to an open site about two miles east of Nettuno. The 56th Evacuation Hospital established itself here on its arrival on 28 January, and

Nurses filling sandbags.

Daylight bombing raid on Nettuno, 7 February 1944.

the 93rd and 95th Evacuation Hospitals and the 33rd Field Hospital relocated to the same area over the next two or three days. Still under observation from German spotters in the Alban Hills, the bombardment continued throughout the next months.

On 7 February a German aircraft attempting to escape from a pursuing Spitfire jettisoned its bombs over the 95th Evacuation Hospital. The bombs landed on the surgical section and killed twenty-six patients and staff, including two medical officers and three nurses. Sixty-four other personnel were wounded, including the hospital commander. Faced with this loss which rendered the Hospital ineffective, the decision was taken to replace the 95th with the 15th Evacuation Hospital. Previously stationed near Cassino, this unit arrived on 10 February. On the same day, the 33rd Field Hospital came under artillery fire, which killed two nurses and one enlisted man, and wounded a further eleven personnel. The nurses had been off-duty when the attack happened; one was visiting the other's tent to borrow a book when a shell hit. The operating theatre electrical generator was also hit, plunging the tent into darkness and catching it alight. Forty-two patients were evacuated by torchlight, an act which earned four nurses (First Lieutenant Mary Roberts, and Second Lieutenants Elaine Roe, Virginia

Casualties being transferred from an LCI to a hospital ship.

Rourke, and Ellen Ainsworth) the Silver Star, the first to be awarded to women in the US Army. Second Lieutenant Ainsworth's medal was awarded posthumously – she died from wounds sustained in the attack, and is buried in the American Cemetery in Nettuno.

The decision to move the American hospitals out of the town

Allied hospital ships steaming into the harbour of Anzio. These two ships and a third ship were bombed in a night attack late in January during which HMHS *St David* was sunk.

buildings was correct: both Anzio and Nettuno were reduced to rubble, and the original locations were not sufficiently high enough above the water table to permit digging proper trenches. In the new, inland, site this problem did not exist, and following a series of attacks on both American and British hospitals they were entrenched to give as much protection as possible.

In the British hospital near the Via Anziate the tents could not withstand the heavy February rain. The ground underfoot became a sea of mud, which together with the icy wind made the odds on survival even lower for the wounded men undergoing treatment. Having spent days in combat in the bad weather, without sleep and often without food – hot or cold – and enduring considerable stress, they were not at their fittest even before becoming casualties. Now wounded, they had a further period of delay in the poor hospital conditions before receiving attention. On average, during the height of the battle, soldiers waited seven hours for operations because of the numbers waiting. For the medical staff sleep became a luxury, and one surgeon performed fourteen major operations overnight, followed by another twelve after a few hours' sleep.

On 12 February both hospital areas were bombed, and the British again on 17 and 19 February; on 17 March the British 141st Field Ambulance suffered fourteen killed and seventy-five wounded. Five days later the 15th Evacuation Hospital was hit by shellfire which killed five and wounded fourteen. Convinced that these attacks were deliberate, General Truscott ordered the engineers to improve the defences. Tents were dug in to a depth of three or four feet – as deep as possible given the drainage problems - and earthen revetments erected around them to a height of five feet above ground level, supported by stakes and chicken wire. Within the tents sandbags divided the bed spaces into groups of ten, so that the effects of hits would be minimised. The operating theatres were roofed with two-inch thick timbers covered with sandbags.

Notwithstanding these improvements, which undoubtedly saved lives, the hospitals continued to suffer casualties from enemy action. There was no 'rear area' at Anzio, and the hospital area became known as 'Hell's Half-Acre' to the troops, many of whom – even when wounded – considered themselves safer in the front line. With manpower depleted by a steady run of casualties, both British and American medical units rotated with those on the Cassino front.

At the beginning of the campaign all casualties were evacuated to Naples, the intention being that they be transported by hospital ship. As the numbers of wounded mounted, LSTs were also pressed into service as casualty carriers, but the drain this imposed on medical staff to accompany them necessitated a change in policy. From early March a 400-bed hospital was established to hold patients who were expected to recover within two weeks. By the end of that month, there were about 5,000 American hospital beds in the Anzio area. That this number included 200 for venereal disease treatment indicates some degree of 'normality' – if such a thing were possible - although casualties suffering this form of incapacity would have become infected before they arrived in the beachhead; the opportunity at Anzio was non-existent.

During the course of the campaign the American and British hospital facilities tended a total of 33,128 and 14,700 patients, respectively. In addition, an unknown number of civilians received treatment.

The American Military Cemetery

On the northern side of Nettuno is the American Military Cemetery, established on the site of a temporary wartime cemetery which was opened two days after the landings. After the war, the temporary cemeteries were done away with, and the bodies of the fallen were either repatriated to the United States or moved here. Most of those buried in Nettuno died in the Sicilian and Italian campaigns, up to the fall of Rome; the majority of Americans who died in the fighting thereafter are buried in the American Cemetery in Florence.

Chapter Two

THE FLYOVER AND THE SALIENT – CARROCETO, APRILIA AND CAMPOLEONE

Leave Anzio on the **SS207 Northwards** – the old Via Anziate. The road passes, on the right, the Anzio CWGC Cemetery, not long before the road leaves the suburbs. The cemetery was used from early in the campaign, and is smaller than the Anzio Beach Head War Cemetery which is further up the road, again to the right. The latter cemetery is situated close to the location of a casualty clearing station during the fighting, and many of those buried here would have died when the medical attention they received proved incapable of dealing with their wounds. Both cemeteries are set in pleasant surroundings, the first overlooking the sea in the distance and the second among trees. In the grounds of the Beach Head Cemetery, in the far right-hand corner from the entrance, is a memorial to five Royal Artillery officers of 655 Air Observation Post Squadron who died during the fighting. Their role was to 'spot' for the artillery from small aircraft, a duty which they were able to perform even when the weather proved too much for fighters and bombers to get to Anzio.

Further north along the road, among a cluster of modern buildings and within an avenue of trees, is the Flyover (known to the Americans as the First Overpass) at Campo di Carne, underneath which is a sign recording the fact that thousands of men fought and died here. The road then continues northwards towards the Alban Hills, bending slightly as it, and the railway line which runs to its west, passes under what is today the SS148, the dual carriageway running from Rome to Latina. In 1944 this was a disused railway bed, known to the Allies as the Embankment. Immediately beyond the road tunnel lies the railway station of Carroceto, which today is indistinguishable from the outer edges of the town of Aprilia. In 1944 Aprilia was a much smaller place, which lay a little to the northeast of the station.

Continue **north through the built-up area**. The road skirts the centre of Aprilia which lies to the right, as the ground becomes more rolling and starts to rise to the Alban Hills. As you approach Campoleone, the numbers of buildings begin to increase again, clustered closely on both sides of the road. At the northern end of town, just to the north of a tunnel under the railway line, are traffic lights at a **five-way road junction. Take the turning first right,** which bends back almost parallel to the road up which you have just driven, signposted Cisterna. The road again passes under the railway line, and a short way beyond this takes a turn to the left. At this point, the line of the road down which you have been travelling continues straight ahead, but is now unpaved, at the end of which is a crossroads where the tarmac resumes. Should you wish to take this route, you will have now driven the depth of the salient. The British positions lay to the east and west of the SS207. The road down which you have just come was the ground the Germans crossed when attacking the salient from the east, and the low ground which lies between the road and the buildings of Aprilia was that held by 1st (British) Division.

The drive you have just taken illustrates the distance covered by 1st (British) Division, and the amount of ground which it then had to defend. The division had only progressed part of the way towards the VI Corps' objectives, blocking Routes 6 and 7, and it is appropriate at this point to reflect upon whether or not these objectives were realistic, as the strategic planners believed them to be. Not only were they some distance from the landing beaches, but the lines of communication from Anzio and Nettuno to the Highways would have had to be defended with the limited troops available. 1st Division had to fight hard to extricate itself from the salient without being cut off – how would VI Corps have managed not to become isolated had they pushed into and beyond the Alban Hills? With the customary invaluable gift of hindsight, it is clear that the Fifth Army drive through the Gustav Line could not have relieved them before they were overwhelmed by the enemy.

On 25 January 1944, three days after the landings (and, according to many of the soldiers, not before time) 1st Division moved up the Via Anziate and under the Flyover. At dawn on the previous day a reconnaissance had been made by troops in Bren carriers, which had run into enemy fire at Carroceto. They had also been shelled by 88mm guns when they investigated the

Leading the advance was the 5th Battalion, Grenadier Guards.

buildings in Aprilia, the 'Factory', which was not recorded on the maps they had available to them. Having carried out their mission, the reconnaissance party withdrew, leaving five men missing behind them. 24 Guards Brigade was ordered up to clear Aprilia the following day.

Leading the advance was the 5th Battalion, Grenadier Guards, which they would have regarded as their right as the senior infantry regiment of the British Army. With a group of spectators watching them from the top of the Flyover, which included the Divisional and Brigade Commanders and the Commander Royal Artillery, Number 1 Company of the Grenadiers proceeded towards Carroceto aboard RASC lorries. The remainder of the battalion marched. Behind them, the Scots and Irish Guards waited their turn, and a queue of traffic some two miles long stretched back towards Anzio.

It was not long before the Germans reacted to the movement, and the spectators heard small-arms fire from the north. Shortly thereafter, artillery shells began to range onto the Flyover, killing a military policeman who was standing beneath it. It was the last time for several months that the Flyover could be used with impunity as a grandstand.

The Grenadiers secured the Embankment, to the south of Carroceto, and by late afternoon they were firmly in place in the Factory. The achievement had cost them almost a company's strength.

True to form, the Germans mounted counterattacks that night. Shortly before dawn battle groups of *3rd Panzer Grenadier Division*, supported by a troop of Tiger tanks and a number of self-propelled guns, attacked from the north east and east of the Factory. The weather was inclement – hail and rain – and the Germans were able to move up to within 200 yards of the Grenadiers' positions. The day was spent in hard fighting as the Guards strove to hold the ground they had taken earlier, but they were then able to settle in and to consolidate their gains. Enemy shelling had wrought havoc around the road and rail

Tiger tank operating in Italy.

Knocked out Shermans. Infantry tended to stick close to tanks as they provided cover from bullets and shrapnel. However, tanks also attracted enemy gunners.

bridges under the Embankment, destroying numerous vehicles; nine Shermans were also knocked out by artillery and anti-tank fire, and the Irish Guards suffered over ninety casualties during the day, many because they were deployed close to the tanks which attracted enemy attention.

The second phase of the Division's advance up the road began during the afternoon of 30 January. It was to seize Campoleone, after which 1st (US) Armored would pass through and push north, while the British carried out mopping-up operations between Campoleone and Albano. To the right, 3rd (US) Division was to get astride Highway 7 and then push northwest to the high ground overlooking Velletri. 45th (US) Division would relieve the units on the flanks of the beachhead so that they could take part in the attack.

3 Brigade Group, which had yet to be involved in the battle, was selected to make the assault on Campoleone, supported by 46th RTR, less one squadron. 1st Battalion, King's Shropshire Light Infantry, would capture a point east of the road and just south of the railway line running through Campoleone Station. 1st Battalion, The Duke of Wellington's Regiment would take a

point five hundred yards to the left of the road, about 200 yards short of the railway embankment; then 2nd Battalion, The Sherwood Foresters would pass through to take the crossroads at Osteriaccia, some 1,000 yards north of the railway crossing.

In preparation for the British attack it was necessary to secure a start line for the KSLI, about a mile south of their objective, a task which was to be carried out by the Grenadiers. Hastening forward for an orders group meeting with their commanding officer at the Scots Guards Headquarters, all of the Grenadiers' company commanders, and the intelligence and signals officers, took a wrong turning and ran into an enemy outpost. Three of the company commanders were killed and one was reported missing. This disaster left the Grenadiers critically short of officers, and the task of securing the start line devolved onto the two other Guards' battalions. The attack was postponed for twenty-four hours, a delay which was to have unforeseen consequences for 1st Division.

The Germans were hurriedly bringing up additional troops and armour, and by the time the Scots and Irish Guards were ready to resume the advance the enemy was much better prepared to resist it. The Scots Guards around Dung Farm were to wait for the Irish to move up level with them, and then the two battalions would advance the hundred yards forward to their objective. The move was scheduled to commence at 2300

Medium British artillery supporting an attack.

hours, but because the Dukes were held up in taking over the Irish Guards' positions, it was postponed by forty-five minutes. Apart from the occasional clouds that drifted past, visibility became almost as clear as day as the moon rose.

The Irish Guards drew level with the Scots without incident, and supported by a heavy artillery bombardment set off for their objective. They reached the railway halt about half a mile north west of Dung Farm before the enemy reacted with machinegun and artillery fire. The halt had evidently been registered by the German gunners as a defensive fire task, and they now began to lay down shells on the area. The right-hand platoon of No 2 Company was wiped out, and to add to the company's misery Germans began to appear behind them. The company commander shifted his line of advance to the west, across the railway line, which was the less hazardous route followed by No 1 Company, and joined them on the objective.

To their right, the Scots Guards had a similar experience. The advance started out with little trouble, until the two companies on the left (B and C) ran into thick wire entanglements ten yards short of the objective, which were covered by machinegun fire. The other two companies, Left Flank and Right Flank, had had a comparatively easy time moving up further to the east, and B and C Companies were now diverted to follow in their footsteps. Soon after midnight all four companies were either on, or close to, their objectives.

With both Guards' battalions having to feel their way forward on the outer flanks of their advance, the Germans were left in possession of the Via Anziate and the ground immediately to either side of it. The enemy had been given full warning of the attack, from a set of orders which they had discovered on the body of a British officer who had, like the Grenadiers earlier, driven into their lines in error. The Germans which had appeared behind the advancing Guardsmen were part of the trap laid, in which the enemy were to hold the road strongly and to divide their assailants into two dispersed groups well to either side of it, where they could be isolated and cut to pieces by German armour. Without control of the road, there was no way forward for the Guards' anti-tank weapons or tanks; they would have no support.

The Irish Guards' No 3 Company had started out towards the Vallelata Ridge, further west, but having run into resistance that could have only been overcome with the assistance of armour – which was unavailable – it was tasked with breaking through to Nos 1 and 2 Companies before dawn, now no more than two hours away. It was unable to do so, and there was no alternative but to withdraw the two exposed companies before they were overrun. After delays caused by radio failures, the order to retire was eventually received during the short period between Lance Corporal Holwell, the Royal Signals operator with No 2 Company, repairing his set and being killed by enemy fire.

The route back was swarming with Germans, however, and more than half of the two companies that had set out earlier failed to return. They reorganised behind Dung Farm before taking the position over from the Scots Guards who were moving out to reinforce their own companies further north. These companies, too, were expecting attacks by German tanks, and urgently required support. With the assistance of every available man as escort, and despite enemy fire, six anti-tank guns and an ammunition column made it to the forward companies just in time. As dawn broke, the first German attack commenced on Left Flank Company. It was finally overrun at about 0730 hours; only one wounded officer returned, a day later.

During their advance in the previous night, and in resisting the German attacks throughout the day, the Scots Guards lost three officers and forty-two other ranks killed, and very many more wounded. Together with the Irish Guards they had, however, very nearly succeeded in breaking through the enemy lines. The Germans had a gap between *3rd Panzer Grenadier Division* and *65th Infantry Division* which was some two miles wide, covered only by *Leutnant* Semrau with twenty men and a couple of self-propelled guns and a tank-destroyer. Semrau had been the man who had captured the British orders for the attack earlier, and he was to be awarded the Knight's Cross for his work during the two days.

It was now 3 Infantry Brigade's turn to take up the attack. They were to have used the Start Line which the Guards' battalions had been fighting to secure, and the attack was originally scheduled to commence at 0930 hours on the 30 January. With the Guards still reorganising after their efforts, this time was postponed several times until it finally commenced at 1510 hours. The two battalions tasked to carry

Campoleone Station from the north. In the haze in the distance lies Anzio.

out the attack, the Dukes and the KSLI on the left and right respectively, had spent the night around Carroceto and the Factory, and were now faced with the problem that the Via Anziate, up to the Start Line, was still in enemy hands. It was essential to clear the road, for without it anti-tank support could not be brought forward to support them; C Company of the KSLI and a squadron of tanks managed this task by noon, and the way was now open for the attack to commence.

By 1700 hours the KSLI had reached their objective just short of the railway line, but the Dukes has fallen behind. The battalion had encountered problems with Germans in the farms and houses bordering the Via Anziate north of the Start Line, and had suffered mortar bombardments as they advanced. Nevertheless, by nightfall the two battalions had troops well forward.

Now the Foresters moved up, ready to pass through to take Campoleone on the next day. The Brigade's advance had been generally successful, but it had been delayed; the time gained had been invaluable to the Germans, who had taken advantage of it to rush more troops into the area of Campoleone Station.

The Foresters' attack opened at 1030 hours, with the support of a squadron of tanks from 46th RTR. Apart from vague indications that there were large bodies of enemy ahead, the battalion knew very little of what to expect. A and C Companies were ordered to take the railway line, after which B and D

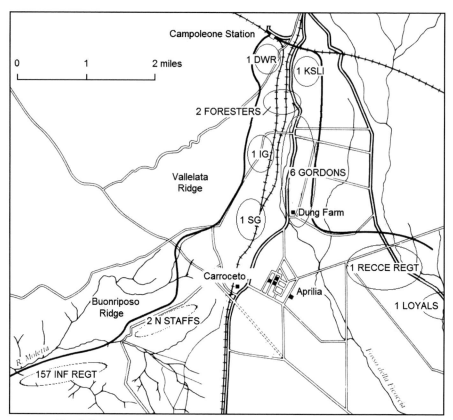

The Salient 30 January.

would pass through and capture the station itself. As the troops advanced they came under merciless fire, and took shelter under the railway embankment. C Company passed through a culvert to the northern side of the embankment, but again came under heavy fire and was forced back the way it had come. A Company, or more accurately its remaining men, crossed the railway line before it, too, was forced to withdraw after taking heavy losses.

Both companies pulled back some 300 yards to allow an artillery bombardment to be brought to bear on the enemy. Then B and D Companies made their attempt to cross the embankment, with no more success than their predecessors. At this stage General Harmon, commander of 1st (US) Armored Division, which was waiting to exploit the advance, came forward to assess the situation. He came forward to the Foresters' position in a tank, before dismounting and walking through the clusters of bodies. On shouting for the Foresters' commanding officer, a 'mud-covered sergeant with a handle-bar moustache' rose from a foxhole and stood stiffly to attention. The Sergeant informed Harmon that sixteen men were left of the 116 that had started out. He had been ordered to hold out until sundown, and thought that, with a little good fortune, that they would be able to do so. But he was not called upon to do so; the Foresters were withdrawn from their hopeless position and the third of the battalion that was left reformed behind the Dukes.

Further east, the Rangers had come to grief south of Cisterna, and the British advance towards Campoleone had run up against an impervious wall of Germans. VI Corps' plans to break out of the beachhead had come to naught, and the initiative was now with the enemy, who set out to destroy the pocket of troops in the salient.

As a start, the *29th Panzer Grenadier Regiment* which had borne the brunt of the fighting against the British, was replaced by a regiment from *715th Infantry Division*, which began to press against the Dukes' positions. To remove the salient *Battle Group Gräser*, which comprised *3rd Panzer Grenadier Regiment, 715th Infantry Division* and with elements of *26th Panzer Division* in support would attack from the east, while *Battle Group Pfeiffer*, comprising a regiment from *65th Infantry Division* and units of *4th Parachute Division*, would attack from the west. The first stage of this operation was for elements of each battle group to converge on the Via Anziate about a mile south of the forward positions of 3 Infantry Brigade, after which it would be eliminated.

The first two days of February passed with comparatively little incident, but during the early afternoon of the 3rd the Dukes were attacked and the enemy repulsed with support from 46th RTR. There was then a lull until 2100 hours, when the Irish Guards were subjected to a five-minute artillery barrage, and then a period of silence. No 3 Company, under the Vallelata Ridge and well apart from the other sub-units, was then set upon by massed infantry attacks, preceded by yet another storm of shells. The radio link back to battalion headquarters went silent, and nothing more was heard.

As the Germans infiltrated between the British positions on the west of the salient, the Gordons discovered that they were facing the same problem on the east. At the point of the salient,

Armour and infantry surrounding the beachhead. Some impression of the mud and weather conditions is apparent in this photograph.

3 Brigade was also experiencing enemy activity. Germans forming up south of the Campoleone railway line for an attack on the KSLI were fired upon, and an attempt to seize a building between the two advanced companies was seen off with a counterattack. But while the brigade was managing to hold its positions, the situation to its south was becoming less secure. With the loss of No 3 Company, the Irish Guards had nothing between their positions and the Scots Guards some distance to the south. At 0430 hours B Squadron, 46th RTR was ordered up to support the Irish Guards, approaching through the Gordons' positions on the east of the salient.

On their way, they discovered that the Gordons were no longer in control of the ground. The Gordons' companies had been well strung out, and were attempting to cover a frontage far too long. At 2300 hours the Germans started to fire ranging shots which were the prelude to a massive bombardment. The skies opened and heavy rain began to fall, and in the darkness and wet the Germans managed to infiltrate two companies behind the Gordons, and had another two in front of them. As dawn began to break, the situation became clearer. The Gordons' B Company, with the squadron of tanks that should have been supporting the Irish Guards and with covering fire from the Reconnaissance Regiment's positions to the southeast, began to clear the enemy out of their positions, taking nearly 200 prisoners as they did so.

Now things took a turn for the worse. A and C Companies, which lay to the north of the battalion's locations, began to withdraw. In doing so, they left the protection of their trenches and were badly cut up by German fire not only from their front, but also from Germans who had slipped through the Irish Guards' lines to their rear. Assuming – wrongly - that a withdrawal had been ordered, D Company also began to fall back, and it, too, came under heavy fire.

With the Gordons' forward company positions overrun, the Irish Guards were now in a desperate situation. Their remaining companies were now in full view of German infantry and armour occupying the ridge to their east. There was little option but to retire, and Nos 1 and 2 Companies, with battalion headquarters and the nine men that remained from the 2/7th Middlesex machinegun platoon that was attached, split into small groups and moved southwards towards No 4 Company.

Headquarters Company ran into the enemy, and – under the muzzles of Spandaus – was compelled to surrender. Marched off with an individual guard for each Guardsman, the Company Commander, Captain Simon Combe addressed his captor politely, stating that he would 'do you in when I get a chance.' As the group came into view on a bank it came under fire, which distracted the Germans. Combe picked up a rifle from the bank and shot his guard. The Germans did not seem to have noticed, so Combe then picked up a Tommy Gun and fired a burst into the nearest group of the enemy. This led to a general attack on the Germans by the rest of the prisoners, resulting in twenty of them being killed and nine being taken prisoner (a tenth was recorded as 'missing', whatever that may have implied).

Throughout that night men managed to slip back behind Dung Farm, until the battalion numbered 270 men. A reinforcement of eighty more allowed three companies to be formed, and the battalion moved to a reserve position behind the Grenadiers and the North Staffordshires, taking up residence in the Caves.

At the top of the salient 3 Brigade was beginning to feel increasingly isolated. Germans were on the Via Anziate south of them, and it was only a matter of time before they were crushed by the enemy forces pressing in on them from all directions.

Help was in the offing, however. 168 Brigade from 56th Division had arrived in the beachhead and was now moved northwards from reserve positions around the Flyover. 1st Battalion, The London Scottish was ordered up on 4 February and with support from the remaining tanks of 46th RTR advanced through what was left of the Gordons towards that battalion's earlier positions northeast of Dung Farm. Their approach was met with firm resistance by the Germans in trenches all around. Pressing on determinedly, they took their objective, but at cost: D Company had only ten men left from the seventy-eight that started the attack.

On the Via Anziate A Company lost all but the company commander and five men in clearing the enemy from the remains of the houses that bordered the road, but the road south for 3 Brigade was open. Orders were given for the brigade's withdrawal. The Dukes would leave at 1715 hours, the KSLI forty-five minutes later, and the Foresters would make their departure half-an-hour after that.

All three battalions had to fight for their freedom, and more casualties were suffered before they were safe – if that is the word – behind Carroceto in the early hours of 5 February. At midnight, the London Scottish, task accomplished, withdrew south of the Factory.

Carroceto

The Germans' attention now turned to the task of clearing the Allies out of their remaining positions north of the Flyover, before driving down the Via Anziate to Anzio itself. Carroceto was the first objective, to be attacked from the north and northeast by *Battle Group Gräser* and from the west by *65th Infantry Division.*

In front of Carroceto was the Factory. During the night of 4/5 February the 1st Battalion, The London Irish had taken over the area, and spent the next two days preparing their defences for the expected enemy attacks. The battalion had already experienced a period of hard fighting on Mount Damiano, further south on the Garigliano front, and needed a draft of ten officers and 250 men to bring them back up to strength. The draft consisted of troops who, for the most part, had not seen action before; nor was there time to absorb them into the regimental ethos – or even for the officers and men to get to know each other, a vital element in creating an effective fighting force. Nor, by this stage of the war, were many of the men Irish, for the reinforcements were drawn from throughout the British Army, including numbers of Gunners from disbanded light anti-aircraft units.

The London Irish had to cover a front nearly a mile long, between the Scots Guards to the west and 10th Battalion, The Royal Berkshire Regiment to the east. What remained of the London Scottish was between the Irish and the Berkshires, and to their rear. As so often at Anzio, there were not enough troops to cover the front adequately, and the company positions were dispersed with no possibility of providing mutual support. Nor was there the possibility of the battalion position having much depth.

The first enemy blows fell on the Irish D Company, north of

The London Irish moving up to the Salient. RHQ Royal Irish Rangers

the Factory, on 6 February. The battered shell of the town itself was too unhealthy a place to deploy troops, apart from a few observers in the tallest buildings, and D Company was somewhat exposed on the slopes leading to its ruins. The Germans got close enough for grenades and bayonets to be used, and both D and B Companies (to the right) came under machinegun fire from weapons that the enemy had succeeded in placing behind the walls of a cemetery which lay in front of the Irish trenches. A request from the commanding officer, Lieutenant Colonel Good, to pull the two companies back from their hopeless positions was refused. The situation – and the Factory - was too critical.

During the afternoon of the following day the artillery again subjected the London Irish to more misery, and German aircraft arrived to strafe their trenches. That night the enemy launched their attacks on the North Staffords on the Buonriposo Ridge off to the west of the Factory, and the Royal Berkshires to the east also came in for their share of German attention. The attack coincided with a handover between two of the Berkshires' companies, and caught men from both sub-units mixed up in the trenches or exposed in the open. The situation was recovered by the commanding officer ordering forward his reserve company and his Bren carriers, which advanced in bright moonlight with their guns firing. The crisis was over here, at least for the moment.

On the Berkshires' right flank B and C Companies came under a sustained assault at about the same time that the carriers had come into action to their west. The German attack almost succeeded in overrunning the positions, but the enemy was seen off by a counterattack which involved every spare man available from the battalion.

On the London Irish front, the enemy began to infiltrate infantry and tanks at about 0135 hours. Contact was lost with D Company, forward of the Factory, an hour-and-a-half later; it had been eradicated. The fighting continued throughout the hours of darkness, and by 0645 hours the right-hand company of the London Irish had been pushed back from east of the Factory. A counterattack failed to restore the situation, and by this time groups of Germans had reached a track about a mile southeast of the Factory. The attack then developed from the northeast, and the easternmost company of the Royal Berkshires appeared to have been overrun. The Germans had control of almost the entire road to the east of the Factory. To the west of the town, they pushed down the railway bed towards Carroceto railway station, where the Scots and Grenadier Guards held their ground.

In and around the railway station buildings was No 4 Company of the Irish Guards. It had been sent forward to support the Scots Guards, who had their headquarters in Carroceto and three companies located north and west of the village. With them was 23rd Field Company, Royal Engineers, acting as infantry.

Throughout the morning of 9 February the pressure was maintained against the Factory, and by 1515 hours the Germans were firmly established in and around the town, with troops from 168 Brigade holding on to houses to its south and southwest. At attempt to retake the town supported by two companies of Sherman tanks from 1st US Armored Division

The Factory, heavily damaged from the fighting.

came to nothing; the enemy had brought up about ten antitank guns to cater for such an eventuality. By this time the bulk of 168 Brigade had withdrawn. Two companies of the London Scottish were about 1,000 yards southeast of the Factory; the London Irish had two companies on the southern edge of the town; and what remained of the Royal Berkshires – little more than a half-company – was withdrawn into reserve between and to the rear of the other two battalions. Their place in the line was taken by an American battalion.

The Scots Guards were fortunate enough to capture a German warrant officer who had the plans for the next German attack in his pocket. At midnight on 9 February *65th Infantry Division* was to attack down the Embankment, while a regiment of *4th Parachute Division* came at Carroceto from the direction of the Vallelata Ridge. Once *29 Panzer Grenadier Regiment* had

The Salient 7 – 10 February.

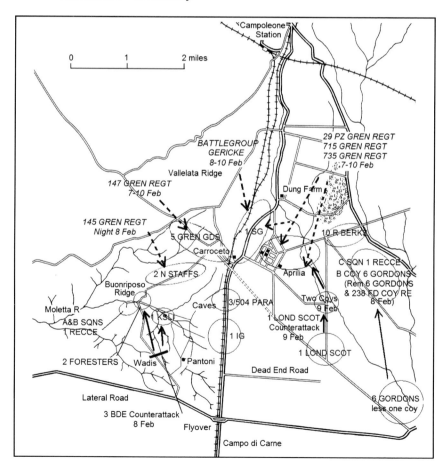

control of the Factory, it, too, would join in the attack, from the east. The Scots Guards responded to this warning by ordering back the forward companies to make a short perimeter around the vital Carroceto bridges, but before they could move, a German Mark IV tank made itself unpleasant outside the battalion headquarters. Despite pleas from the commanding officer, who escaped from the building to fetch help, no Allied armour would move forward to deal with this threat during the hours of darkness, even though several American tank destroyers and Shermans were only 200 yards away. Eventually, the German tank commander appeared to weary of his game and took himself off.

Shortly before dawn battalion headquarters withdrew behind the Embankment, where it joined the Grenadiers' headquarters. By now, communication had been lost with B Company. Right Flank Company, which had been north of the village, was cut off. Some twenty-five Guardsmen managed to escape under cover of a diversion carried out by tanks and tank destroyers, and C Company was also able to fight its way clear.

Of the troops defending the railway station, No 4 Company of the Irish Guards and the company of Sappers, only one platoon of the latter unit escaped. The Irish Guardsmen had held the station and covered the withdrawal of the Scots Guards, until they were assailed by four enemy tanks, two self-propelled antitank guns and paratroops, and were overcome.

The three-day fight for the Factory and Carroceto almost destroyed 1st Division. The Official History gives the effective remaining strength of its battalions as ranging from forty to sixty-five per cent, but other estimates place these as being much lower: between twenty and forty-six per cent at most. The American historian Carlo d'Este regards the performance of these units as being one of the outstanding feats of the war, and their sacrifice was not in vain. The Germans had intended capturing the Factory and Carroceto on 8 February, but did not succeed in doing so until the 11th. The losses inflicted on his own troops were sufficiently heavy to compel von Mackensen to pause and regroup before implementing the next phase of his plan, the drive on Anzio. This delay gave the Allies time to prepare themselves to deal with the threat.

From the standpoint of inter-Allied relationships, things had not gone well. General Penney had repeatedly appealed to

Lucas for urgent reinforcements throughout the three days of the battle, appeals which had been refused. Penney had to defend the indefensible with the minimum of support from Lucas, who just kept reiterating his orders that 1st Division must 'fight it out'. It was not until the morning of 10 February that a decision came from VI Corps Headquarters that 45th US Division would counterattack to retake the Factory; but this could not happen until the following day. The frosty relationship between Penney and Lucas was compounded by the latter's reluctance to leave his cellars in Nettuno to see for himself that the British were fighting a desperate battle. Even when he finally visited the British on 10 February, he did not see the battlefield and therefore still had no understanding of the ground and the conditions under which the troops were existing.

On 11 February the 45th US Division, the 'Thunderbirds', mounted their attempt to retake the Factory, supported by 1st US Armoured Division. They made little headway against the German defenders, and at nightfall they withdrew south of the disused railway bed. No better result was achieved when the attack was renewed the following day, and the Americans established themselves in new positions 500 yards south of the Factory. A lull then fell for the next three days, to be broken by the opening moves of Operation *FISCHFANG*.

Chapter Three

THE WADIS AND THE WESTERN BEACHHEAD

From Anzio take the turn to the right immediately south of the Flyover, which leads to the road running east-west across it, and turn left at the T-junction to cross the Flyover heading west. To the west of the SS207 and the railway line, and to the north of the Flyover, is a post-war industrial complex with four high chimneys. These are visible from several miles away and give a useful reference point when viewing the ground from the Alban Hills, for example.

The road which you have just joined, that crossing the Flyover, was the Allied line of resistance against which the German *FISCHFANG* attack foundered. To the east of the Flyover, the 1st Battalion, The Loyal Regiment had taken up their positions on 10 February; they promptly christened the road 'Wigan Street'. In 1944 the road was bare of trees and with fewer dwellings than today, and looked northwards across flat ground towards the Dead End Road, about 1,100 yards away. Between the two roads there was an area, about 300 yards north of Wigan Street, of dead ground and ditches in which an attacker could assemble his forces unseen.

Comparatively unscathed by the fighting thus far (although the battalion had suffered 137 casualties, the numbers had been replaced by reinforcements) the Loyals now mustered thirty-one officers and 747 men and was the freshest unit in the division. Three of the battalion's four rifle companies were deployed on a 1,000-yard front along Wigan Street: A Company was in the Flyover area, B Company around Carne Farm, north of the road, and C Company further east in a group of houses. D Company provided a degree of depth to the position, being situated south of the road, to the east of a building christened 'Todhunter Lodge'.

When the battalion took up these positions, the possibility that they might have to defend them appeared remote, but as the days passed and the Germans pressed further southwards, the situation changed. By noon on 17 February enemy tanks could be seen near the Dead End Road, and artillery rounds began to land around the Flyover, through which casualties had been moving southwards for several hours.

As the survivors of the fighting in the Salient withdrew, they took up their places to defend the line of the Lateral Road. 179 US Infantry Regiment was to the east of the Loyals, the Gordons to their west. Behind them were the North Staffordshires, and yet further back again were the assortment of units, sub-units and scratch-platoons that formed up on the various defensive positions between the Lateral Road and the sea. The main German thrust, however, was to be down the Via Anziate through the Flyover, and it was here that the Loyals stood.

It was not long before the enemy arrived. After a night of artillery bombardment, B Company was attacked at 0500 hours on 18 February. One of their forward platoons vanished under the onslaught; the Germans suddenly appeared behind Loyal lines – Todhunter Lodge was in their hands; and A Company was under attack. C Company was able to recover the Lodge before having to return to its position on the road to repel yet another attack. The line held, as did that on either side of the battalion, and during the early afternoon D Company recovered

The Flyover 18 – 20 February.

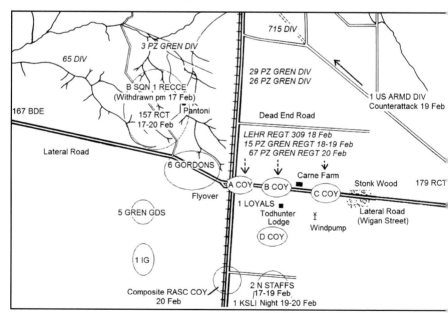

150

The Flyover, known to the Americans as the 'First Overpass', after the battles for Anzio.

those positions which B Company had lost earlier in the day.

At 1700 hours A Company again came under heavy attack, this time by a whole German battalion. The battle took place at close quarters, with hand-to-hand fighting and grenades, and continued for an hour before the enemy retired. A Company had been supported in its fight by a company of Gordons from their left, and by some tanks, but was reduced to fifty men. C Company was down to sixty. Quartermaster staff, cooks, drivers and every other available soldier were pressed into service with the rifle companies to man the line.

In support, a company of the 2/7th Middlesex Regiment – the machinegun battalion of the 1st Division – was able to fire right across the front. One of its platoons fired 32,000 rounds during the day, and it was estimated that six Germans fell for every one that made it to the British trenches. The enemy casualties were shattering, but they persevered with great determination and courage.

During the evening the Loyals' A Company came under renewed attack, and then at 0400 hours the following morning C Company and 1/179th Infantry Regiment were stormed. C Company was overrun, and the Germans turned their attention westwards along Wigan Street to B and D Companies. By 0600 hours they had managed to break a hole in the Loyals' line. The only troops immediately on hand to counter this threat was No 2 Company of the Staffords, which counterattacked at 1100 hours, supported by every available gun and a smoke screen. The Staffords came under heavy machinegun fire and lost all of the company officers and most of the NCOs, and the attack ground to a halt 150 yards short of the objective.

The Staffords' No 1 Company, supported by flanking fire from D Company of the Loyals and from tanks, resumed the counterattack at 1500 hours, in a heavy thunderstorm. As they worked their way towards the objective they were surprised to see parties of Germans emerging with their hands raised in surrender, escorted by Loyals who had turned the tables on their captors. The infection of defeat spread, firstly through the enemy troops on the objective, and then right along the Loyals' front; and the British made haste to take advantage of the situation before any German minds could be changed. The enemy's collapse was total, and their offensive was broken; but at a cost to the Loyals of over 200 casualties on 19 February alone.

Continue westwards, on what was known as the Lateral Road in 1944, and take the first turning right, about a mile away from the Flyover. The branch road runs through the wadi area, but little can be seen of them until you are on the hillside overlooking a quarry in the valley to the right of the road. Parking on the roadside here is possible, but with care: the local drivers can prove intimidating as they speed by.

Through the valley below you runs one of the streams running into the Moletta River. It has gentle banks where the road crosses it, but much steeper ones only a short distance upstream, where it passes through a deep cutting which today has trees and scrub growing in it, and by which you can trace its route from where you stand. The barrier that this gully, or wadi in the British Army parlance of the time, presents to both vehicles and infantry is not readily apparent until one stands on its lip.

The wadis extend back southwards almost as far as the Lateral Road and the Flyover. To the west of where you stand, they stretch to the Moletta River and beyond – the tributaries of that drainage feature are what carved them. The streams cut gullies through the ground, which have steep sides in places forty or more feet deep, difficult to climb especially when slick with rainfall. At the bottom, the water may be a couple of feet deep, or virtually non-existent, depending upon the season and the weather, and the wadis twist and turn as they progress. The impression when clambering through them is one of moving through claustrophobic narrow alleyways between high buildings, with little or no chance of knowing what danger lies around the next corner and no easy way of escaping it; the sides are too steep and greasy and the bottom often too waterlogged to permit sufficiently swift movement to avoid a burst of fire or a hail of grenades. On all too many occasions, for all of those who fought in these unpleasant conditions, moving around a bend was the last thing they did. Individuals and sections of troops disappeared – it was a particularly close-range and personal war which wore on the nerves of those involved.

The wadis were christened with a variety of titles – 'The Boot' and 'The Lobster Claw', for example, from their appearance on the map or from aerial photographs. Another was 'The

An aerial view of part of the Wadis.

Fortress', after which Raleigh Trevelyan named his account of his time there. Just below the Buonriposo Ridge, which extends on the far side of the stream before you, are the remnants of the area known in 1944 as 'The Caves'. Here the streams and human endeavour in bygone times had carved tunnels through the ground, some of them large enough to conceal vehicles. Vestiges of them can be seen on the right of the road on the far side of the valley, beyond the quarry.

On 30 January 1944, as part of General Lucas' move

'The Boot' today.
Part of the Caves area today

Sherman tanks moving inland.

to expand the beachhead, Combat Command A of the 1st US Armored Division advanced to the left of the 1st Division's drive up the Via Anziate. The intention was for General Harmon's Americans to encircle Campoleone from the west, while the British drove through Carroceto and Aprilia. Harmon intended to send his tanks north-west along the disused railway embankment which lay immediately south of Carroceto. Before this could happen, however, his troops had to capture part of the embankment on which they could establish their start line.

The American advance for this first step was carried out without the benefit of reconnaissance, which – had it happened – would have relegated the plan to the dustbin, for it was to be carried out across the wadis. Invisible to the observer more than a few yards away on the ground, from aircraft they appeared to be no more than hedgerows. They form a tank barrier which cannot be traversed without bridging equipment. So much for the intelligence appreciation which described the area as 'undulating country, thickly intersected by shallow streams which, even in wet weather, would exercise only a delaying influence on armour.'

The first elements of the American force moved northwards to the Flyover before going westwards for about a mile. They then turned north again, towards the Buonriposo Ridge. Shortly afterwards, their advance came to a halt when the ground proved impassable to tanks – the seemingly solid surface was no more than a sea of mud, and the lead tank and a half-track bogged-down. The Germans quickly brought 88mm fire onto them; the attack was unable to progress and was abandoned.

This brief and relatively inglorious episode was far from being the only fighting in the area, however. As described elsewhere, 1st Division forced a deep salient as far north as Campoleone Station, which was fiercely counterattacked by the Germans who attempted to cut through its base to isolate, and then destroy, the units at its apex. The area in front of you now was the western shoulder of the salient, and had the enemy been able to drive through it they would have been successful in their intention of slicing it off. Between the Germans and their objective stood both British and American forces.

The Buonriposo Ridge was occupied on 1 February by the 2nd Battalion of the North Staffordshire Regiment. Two companies, A and B, were positioned forward, with the remaining two situated in depth to the rear, and battalion headquarters below the crest of the hill. The ground in front of the battalion positions was covered by scrub which concealed enemy movement, in places right up to and between the forward company positions. After some days of increasing enemy artillery and mortar fire the front went quiet on 5 February until the 7th, when after nightfall the Germans began probing towards the 3/157th US Infantry Regiment, off to the Staffords' left.

Then a Stafford outpost was rushed by the enemy, a precursor to German infiltration between the company positions. Moving into the wadis and gullies, covered by the scrub, they attacked C Company in the rear of the battalion positions before pushing even deeper and engaging the mortar platoon in hand-to-hand combat. Having driven the enemy off at the point of the bayonet, the mortar teams retired in the direction of the battalion headquarters once their ammunition state ran low, taking the sights from their weapons with them.

The forward companies, A and B, now found themselves with the enemy at all sides. B Company was totally cut off, and was reduced to about thirty men. They reduced their defensive perimeter and then tried – unsuccessfully – to move back onto the battalion headquarters. A Company, down to some twenty

German paratroops working their way through the Moletta River area.

men, fired a volley at close range into a group of Germans who had stumbled across them, before they withdrew.

The situation was grave. In battalion headquarters the commanding officer, Lieutenant Colonel Snodgrass, with the adjutant and the regimental sergeant major, collected the stragglers as they fell back. For some hours they held off the Germans, before at about 0300 hours the survivors pulled back to the Via Anziate, suffering more casualties as enemy shells fell amongst them. Nearly three-quarters of the battalion had been lost by dawn.

In the Caves below the Ridge, the Irish Guards were now the only Allied troops blocking the Germans from the main road. No. 1 Company had been ordered forward to support the Staffords, but had encountered the enemy en route. Only twenty men returned to the Caves, having been separated from the rest of the company in the wadis. Nothing was known of the fate of the remaining Guardsmen until the German propaganda machine later announced the names of a few prisoners.

On the Staffords' left flank, the Ridge was held by the 3rd Battalion of 157 (US) Infantry Regiment, from the 45th Division. The German attack thrust between the Staffords and the Americans' L Company; an enemy machinegun crew got inside the American positions before being dealt with by a party from K Company. The fighting swung back and forth as positions were lost and regained. Having got through the Staffords' front, enemy troops moved west and engaged the 3/157th from the right rear with tank and small-arms fire. The Battalion Commander, Major Boyd, was killed and Captain Mitchell, the Executive Officer, assumed command. He withdrew L Company south of the Ridge and re-aligned his right flank to the southeast to counter the German threat, which saved the battalion but – together with the overrunning of the Staffords' positions - allowed the enemy to take the Ridge.

The amount of defensive artillery fire brought down by the Americans' supporting batteries was immense: during the two days' fighting on 7 and 8 February, over 25,000 shells were fired on 3/157th Regiment's front. The Regiment used three days' machinegun ammunition supplies and more than 9,200 mortar bombs, but the German military machine kept advancing.

To the right of the positions held earlier by the North Staffords on the Buonriposo Ridge, 5th Battalion Grenadier Guards held the line of the Embankment. Here, too, the relatively quiet days before the battle concealed the German preparations as they slipped forward through the gullies and undergrowth. When the assault opened on the Staffords, the Grenadiers came under attack from all directions, the enemy having slipped between the platoon positions. No 3 Company was overrun within the space of an hour, and only the company commander and nine men made it safely to the position held by No 1 Company. The strength of the two combined companies was quickly reduced to about fifty men, and as ammunition was running low, they withdrew towards No 2 Company, further down the Embankment.

Their retreat was hindered by the surrounding Germans, with further losses inflicted on their dwindling numbers. To add to the Grenadiers' woes, No 4 Company came under attack from the rear, by Germans who had penetrated the Staffords' positions before swinging eastwards behind the Buonriposo Ridge. This company, too, suffered heavy casualties and only a few men made it safely to battalion headquarters.

In summary, within a few hours of the start of the German attack the remaining Grenadiers were clustered around the Carroceto bridges. No 2 Company was still on the Embankment, maintaining a tenuous link with the Scots Guards to their right. A mixed group of men from Headquarters and Support Companies, with anyone who could be found to bear arms, was in a gully about 300 yards west of the Via Anziate. Battalion Headquarters was separated from No 2 Company by Company H of 504 Parachute Infantry Regiment. And to the south lay the Irish Guards, who were attempting to plug the gap left by the Staffords. The Grenadiers were to lose over 300 officers and men – including their third commanding officer within twelve days – in three days of fighting.

The Via Anziate, as so often during the Anzio saga, was the crucial point in this particular stage of the battle; and at this moment all depended upon control of the Carroceto bridges which lay across it. Were the Germans able to capture them, then the road would be open to the sea, with only minimal

The Carroceto underpass after the battle.

Allied forces left to attempt to halt them. To the north, the London Irish were still in possession of the Factory despite enemy troops percolating into its western and southern edges. There was a gap between the London Irish and the Scots Guards, but the Scots and the Grenadiers' No 2 Company were firmly holding the area of the bridges. The danger lay behind them, from the direction of Buonriposo Ridge, which was now open.

Between the main road and the enemy lay the gully – 'Grenadier Gully' – in which were assembled the miscellany of Guards' sub-units and American paratroops. As the advancing Germans struggled to cross a bramble-infested ditch, steep-sided and knee-deep in water, the Allied troops opened a concentrated fire which delayed them until they discovered a narrow footpath through the obstacle. Now able to advance unhindered by natural barriers, they ran into a small group of Grenadiers under the command of Major William Sidney, the Support Company commander. As the enemy approached, Sidney engaged them with his Tommy Gun, until it jammed. He then proceeded to throw grenades at any German bold enough to expose himself. Two Guardsmen supported him, priming grenades and passing them forward as fast as they could, until a grenade detonated prematurely, killing on of them and wounding Sidney in the back. Despite his injuries, which were added to when fragments from a German stick grenade struck his face, Major Sidney kept up the fight until the Germans had decided that enough was enough. He was awarded the Victoria Cross for his gallantry, which had kept the enemy from pushing through to the road.

By the morning of 8 February, the Buonriposo Ridge was in enemy hands. The survivors from the Staffords (such as they were, the battalion having lost twenty-three officers and 300 men in the eight hours since the German attack opened) were fighting in scattered groups and as individuals alongside the Grenadier and Irish Guards and American paratroops, or were back to the south of the Flyover. The battalion headquarters of the Grenadiers was still in the Gully, with No 2 Company on the Embankment; and the remaining Irish Guardsmen and 3/504th Parachute Infantry were blocking the route from Buonriposo to Via Anziate. This last position was still the most dangerous one, for should the enemy penetrate it, then the whole of 1st

Division's defence would crumble. General Penney was therefore compelled to commit his last reserve, 3 Infantry Brigade, in an attempt to retake the Ridge.

3 Brigade had been positioned south of the Flyover, prepared to counterattack as ordered. It had spent the night of 7/8 February moving forth and back as the enemy threatened various spots, and few men had any rest. Finally, the 1st Battalion, King's Shropshire Light Infantry and the 2nd Battalion, Sherwood Foresters, with a squadron of tanks from 46th RTR in support, were told off for an attack on Buonriposo Ridge, to commence at 1130 hours. This gave little time for the KSLI to move across from their positions east of the Flyover, and the attack was postponed, firstly by an hour and then to 1300 hours to allow them to take up their places. Unfortunately the artillery barrage, timed for the 1230 hours' attack, could not be called off and the enemy were given ample warning of the impending assault.

The Foresters had been on their start line for two hours, awaiting the arrival of the KSLI. During this time they had been shelled regularly. The Start Line straddled the road, stretching to

British troops taking cover in a ditch on the beachhead.

both east and west, which runs northwards from the Lateral Road and which you drove down earlier. In 1944 it passed through open countryside which was cut through by the deep wadis. As the KSLI hurriedly assembled and advanced to this line, they had to cross about 5,000 yards of ground, half of it in full view of the enemy. Once committed to the attack, they again came into enemy view after some 100 yards of leaving the Start Line, when both battalions were subjected to an intense bombardment until they were able to take cover in the wadis stretching across their front. All of the officers from the KSLI's B and C Companies were casualties. The non-commissioned officers took control and led the surviving troops through the twisting wadis to the Fosso di Carroceto. Now they were faced with an uphill slope to the top of the ridge, swept by machinegun fire from the flanks. The KSLI could not advance through this, and the assault came to a halt.

To their left, the Foresters had to advance without the benefit of the cover afforded by the wadis. Their path was less well cut-up by these obstacles, but by the same token, there was less opportunity to shelter from the enemy fire. The battalion's movement continued forward as its numbers steadily decreased. By mid-afternoon, the remaining thirty-five men of A Company reported back that they were secure on their objective, with B Company stationed to their rear. Of C Company, there was no information until later, when it became clear that the entire complement was killed, wounded or missing. Without the KSLI in place to give support, the Foresters could not hold their position, and they fell back to a position around a farmhouse. Tank support, once again because of the problems of advancing across this country, was of little help.

That night, 8 February, the two battalion headquarters were co-located in a house short of their objectives, with many of their men still in the wadis. While the wadis may have offered shelter from enemy fire, they did not from the freezing rain which started to fall, causing the streams which ran through them to rise knee-high, and adding to the discomfort of the battered infantrymen. The sacrifice of the two battalions had been great, but it did prevent the Germans from cutting into the divisional flank from the west. For the time being, the position was secure.

For the German planners, there were two routes forward

through this area to the Flyover. The first was from the Buonriposo Ridge along the road which ran to the west of the Lobster Claw, which met the Lateral Road a mile or so to the west of the Flyover; the second was from the Ridge, across the Fosso di Carroceto and then southeast before turning south through the small number of buildings which were known as Pantoni, and then joined the first route just north of its junction with the Lateral Road. It is here that the British and American troops fought a desperate battle which became known as the 'War of the Wadis'.

The remnants of the KSLI and the Foresters fell back around Pantoni after the failed attempt to retake the Ridge. Supporting them was a platoon of the 2/7th Middlesex Regiment with their machineguns. Now, on 14 February, renewed German attacks began. After an uncertain start – the Germans seemed unsure of the defenders' positions – the assault firmed up, but came to grief on the belt of barbed wire which the British had erected across their front and on which the machinegunners concentrated their fire.

In the beachhead 167 Brigade from the 56th (London) Division was now available to support 1st Division. 8th and 9th Battalions of the Royal Fusiliers relieved 157 (US) Infantry, to the west of the KSLI and Foresters, and the remnants of these two battered battalions were relieved by 7th Battalion, The Oxfordshire and Buckinghamshire Light Infantry. 45th (US) Infantry Division took over the defences across the Via Anziate, with 2/157th Infantry Regiment in the Caves.

The Ox and Bucks' introduction to Anzio was unwelcoming. The battalion moved into the wadis during the night hours, and had the following day to settle in before the next round of attacks commenced in the evening. After being bombed by aircraft and subjected to an artillery barrage, it was assaulted by waves of German infantry. Communications were lost with C Company, positioned forward, and it was presumed to have been overrun by the enemy; at 1100 hours A Company was also reported overrun, and one of D Company's platoons lost. The remainder of the battalion was under heavy attack. The commanding officer had been wounded and evacuated before the battalion had moved forward, and the second-in-command was killed during the afternoon. The senior officer in the headquarters was now the adjutant, Captain Close-Brooks, who ordered the survivors to fall back onto his position, where they determined to hold out in a hollow in the ground protected by wire and mines. The remaining company, B, was off to the right of the headquarters group, but communications failed during the middle of the afternoon and it, too, was assumed lost. Behind the headquarters the battalion mortar sections were outflanked by the Germans and forced to abandon their weapons; only seven men managed to join the beleaguered headquarters group.

To the west, the Fusilier battalions came under attack at dawn. German troops which had infiltrated between the company positions during the night overran the rear companies and pushed a hole in the defences. By evening, the 8th and 9th Fusiliers had each lost their two forward companies. The front of 167 Brigade was reduced to little more than the headquarters of the Ox and Bucks, with the remnants of two companies from 8th Fusiliers and one company of the 9th. Together with scratch parties of drivers, clerks and anyone else who could be cobbled together, this was all that stood between the enemy and the Lateral Road. What was left of the London Scottish and the London Irish was rushed across to provide a skimpy stop line to the north of the road, but even now a gap remained which could only be covered by artillery fire.

On 16 February Operation *FISCHFANG* opened. Clearing the Allied troops north of the Flyover was the first phase of the German plan, to be carried out by *3rd Panzer Grenadier Division*. In support, *65th Infantry Division* was to advance from the Buonriposo Ridge. Directly in their path lay 2/157th (US) Infantry Regiment, which had taken over the Caves during the previous evening. At 0730 hours the enemy fell upon E Company, situated just south of the Carroceto bridges, and overran the left-hand platoon. An American tank destroyer knocked out two German tanks, and shot up their infantry with its machine guns. Throughout the day the American battalion came under continuous attacks as the enemy pressed them from both the north and from across the Via Anziate to their east; eventually the Germans managed to put men into the gully behind them, thus virtually cutting them off. Isolated, the nearest Allied troops to them were the Ox and Bucks, about a mile west of their positions.

As the battle progressed, both sides took heavy casualties, a factor which led to one of those instances in warfare of almost civilised behaviour. At about 1100 hours, a German half-track bearing a white flag appeared before E Company, from which a German officer emerged to propose a thirty-minute ceasefire to evacuate all of the wounded. Captain Sparks, the American company commander, agreed, and both sides collected their casualties. About twenty Americans were loaded into a truck and sent rearwards, and then Sparks called down artillery fire onto his own position to deal with the enemy which were again threatening him.

That night Captain Sparks, his company now down to fifty-strong from its original number of nearly 200 men, returned to the rear and collected two Sherman tanks, the only ones still running from the platoon that he had been promised. They were a welcome reinforcement, but his dwindling company was hard-pressed. An attempt to move I Company forward in

British and American prisoners carrying stretchers, with their German guards.

support of the 2/157th came to nothing. Firstly, confusion led to the company being ordered back to its original position south of the Flyover, and then it came under attack from butterfly bombs, which inflicted several casualties.

At midnight on 16 February the 2/157th managed to make contact with the Ox and Bucks; although there was now some hope that the flank had been made secure the pressure was still on. E Company continued to lose men. A company from 725 Grenadier Regiment infiltrated Sparks' defences and killed or captured the men in his outposts.

Before dawn on 17 February the Germans laid down another artillery barrage before launching another attack down the Via Anziate. On the eastern and western flanks the Allied line held, but sagged in the centre, the enemy pushing a two-mile wide front stretching from the Caves almost to Padiglione village, down to the Lateral Road. 2/157th was left projecting into the enemy lines, with the Germans pressing southwards on either side of its positions and driving the defenders back. The battalion steadily withdrew to the area of the Caves, which offered comparative security. E Company was now down to eighteen men, but it was still supported by the two Shermans which gave covering fire as the infantrymen retired. Two companies (H and G) positioned themselves on the ridge in front of the Caves, other sub-units – including the headquarters and the medical staff, set up inside the Caves themselves.

The Caves were already occupied by at least fifty Italian refugees from Aprilia and the surrounding farms, and now the Americans joined them. Comparatively well protected, they were able to bring artillery fire down on the enemy infantry and tanks which attacked them during the night of the 17th.

The Germans maintained their attacks during the following days, at times engaging in hand-to-hand combat at the Caves' mouths. The *65th Infantry Division* employed flame-throwing tanks and even tear gas in attempts to winkle out the defenders, but although they inflicted casualties and took some prisoners, they did not succeed in driving the Americans out. The position was becoming increasingly desperate as numbers of men and vital supplies ran low, and 2/7th Battalion, The Queen's Regiment attempted to relieve the 2/157th during the night of 21 February, but lost seventy-six men from its already depleted numbers, together with much of its supplies and support

An unexploded 'Butterfly Bomb' at Anzio.

weapons, in breaking through - a German aircraft dropped its load of butterfly bombs on the battalion. The Commanding Officer of the 2/157th, Lieutenant Colonel Lawrence Brown, decided to wait another day before retiring. His decision was to lose him one of his platoons, which was forced to surrender when the Germans got into one of the Caves on the 22nd.

The Wadis

At 0200 hours on 23 February, 2/157th made its breakout. Starting out in orderly fashion, and taking the walking wounded with them, the battalion ran into a German position and suffered yet more casualties before reaching British lines. The wounded men that had remained behind were evacuated under a truce with the enemy, but were then taken prisoner.

2/7th Queens, now in the Caves but with little ammunition, food or water, were in an impossible situation. 2/6th Queens were sent forward to support them, but could not get through, and a proposed airdrop of supplies was cancelled because of the weather. On 23 February two of the battalion's companies in the Caves were overrun; the remaining troops attempted to work their way back to Allied lines in small groups, but most were killed or captured. The Germans now had control of the Caves area.

To the west of the Caves area, the war fought by the British battalions during this period had been equally fraught. Here the 8th and 9th Battalions, The Royal Fusiliers, were supported by the London Scottish in their positions to the left and rear of the 2/157th Infantry. To the Fusiliers' right was the Ox and Bucks.

The Ox and Bucks, like the 2/157th, were regularly isolated in their position which blocked the German route through Pantoni and to the Lateral Road. After a delivery of supplies and

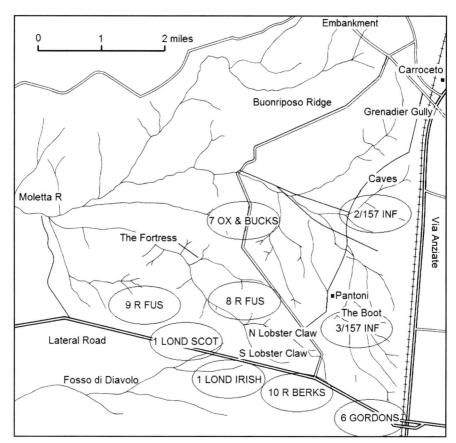

By this date, however, the German offensive had ground to a halt.

ammunition on 18 February, nothing reached the battalion until three days later when a tank broke through, loaded with a minimum of essentials.

Fortunately for the battalion, German attacks on the position were uncoordinated and not pushed home. On the evening of 20 February word came that the London Irish was on the way to relieve it. In fact, the Irish had been trying to do so for the past three days. The Irish, with the other battalions of 168 Brigade, the London Scottish and the Royal Berkshires, had been stationed south of the Lateral Road ready to deal with any attempt by the enemy to get to the Flyover and the Via Anziate from the west. All three battalions were exhausted from their earlier exertions, and were very weak: the London Irish had experienced an eighty per cent turnover of officers and men since the end of January. Although sufficient reinforcements had arrived to allow the battalion to form three rifle companies there had been little time to assimilate the new men into the regiment. Some of them had no time to do more than learn the names of their platoon and section commanders when the battalion was ordered to relieve the Ox and Bucks on 17 February.

A problem faced the Irish: the Ox and Bucks' position was far from clear, and reaching and relieving them was not as simple a task as it might have appeared. The way forward to the assumed location, somewhere on the track leading to the Buonriposo Ridge, lay across the deceivingly flat ground which was cut up by the wadis. To take advantage of the cover that these offered, a circuitous route forward was planned. At first, enemy reaction to the advance was limited to desultory shellfire, and the troops gained the wadis without serious hindrance; once in them, however, movement slowed as they struggled through the brambles and undergrowth and across waterways. They worked their way across the Lobster Claws and the La Cogna wadi, but when they crested the far side they were met by heavy artillery, mortar and small-arms fire from the Germans firmly established in front of them. Casualties were particularly heavy amongst the officers and senior NCO's – a particular problem because of the newness of many of the soldiers to the battalion. A degree of confusion and disorganisation occurred, and it was decided that no further move would be made until darkness fell.

That night patrols were sent forward, but none could find the Ox and Bucks where they were expected to be. The following day, the London Irish tried again, but with no better result that to lose yet more men. By this stage, both A and C Companies were down to about thirty-five men each, and the Commanding Officer – who had had little or no sleep for days – was ordered by the Brigade Commander to hand over to the second-in-command and to take a rest.

It was eventually established that the headquarters and part of one company of the Ox and Bucks were holding out in a ditch about 400 yards from the Irish position in the wadi. To extricate them, brigade headquarters devised a plan wherein the Irish would mount an attack on the end of a wadi held by German paratroops, who were blocking the escape route of the Light Infantrymen. Captain Crozier, now in command of the thirty or so men of C Company, was tasked with carrying out this operation. His small group set off with the intention of clearing out the enemy after encircling them from the left. They were not seen again. Some years later it emerged that they had run into the main enemy positions and were all killed or captured. The Ox and Bucks remained cut off.

As the days progressed, the London Irish were steadily whittled away by German efforts to break through – two Tiger tanks penetrated to a position half a mile behind the battalion's location, but could approach no closer because of the ground, before being driven off; German infantry infiltrated through the wadis; and the Irish were subjected to more mortar and artillery bombardments. They were determined, however, to make another attempt to extricate the Ox and Bucks. One more attack was planned in which the London Irish, now reduced to one company formed from the survivors of the original four rifle companies and a second from headquarters' staff and a miscellany of drivers, together with the London Scottish and a troop of tanks in support, would make the effort.

A two-stage attack was mounted in which an Irish platoon captured an enemy-held building known as 'O.P. House', after which a second platoon passed through and, with the aid of a tank, mopped up the German paratroops. The Ox and Bucks were able to retire, safe at last.

The Ox and Bucks may have been out of harm's way – at least for the time being – but the London Irish were not. The Germans were quick to resume their infiltrations, and that night, after another artillery bombardment, the paratroops retook O.P. House and set up a machinegun on the position. A spirited counterattack across 450 yards of open ground by a section led by Corporal Hill regained the building. Even the Regimental Aid Post was penetrated by the Germans. Their demand that the London Irish surrender had been met with a robust defence from the Medical Officer of the Royal Berkshires, a Czech, who harangued the senior paratroop NCO on the contents of the Geneva Convention, in fluent German. The NCO apologised and withdrew his men.

A second group of paratroops which arrived on the next day was less easily convinced, however. Those in the RAP were taken prisoner, and the Germans began bringing in their own wounded for treatment. An agreement was reached that each side would evacuate their casualties to their respective lines, but

The Fortress. This photograph was evidently taken during one of the rare moments when the area was not subjected to German fire.

the return route for the Germans was impassable. The opportunity was taken for a section of the London Irish to rush the position and to reverse the situation, taking a number of enemy prisoners.

The London Irish remained in the line until they were pulled back to Anzio for re-embarkation to the Naples area on 11 March, with the rest of 56th Division. In six weeks at Anzio the battalion suffered thirty-two officers and 550 other ranks killed, wounded and missing. Only twelve officers and 300 men left the beachhead, many of them only just returned from hospital.

The failure of *FISCHFANG* to break the Allied lines did not halt the warfare on the western flank of the beachhead. Never a suitable route for armour, particularly during the winter months, the fighting here was usually close-quarter infantry combat. Troops from both sides lived their lives, and sometimes died, in the wadis, the gullies, ditches and trenches, and experienced difficulty in moving during the daylight hours. It was this problem of movement that led both sides to discount the area as the most opportune terrain for getting into, or out of,

171

Italian Folgore – paratroops – who remained faithful to the Fascist cause after the surrender of Italy, and who served alongside the Germans on the western beachhead.

the beachhead. To get to the Fortress, for example, troops had to undergo a night march in the depth of the connecting wadis and trenches holding fast to the belts of the men in front as they stumbled through the blackness, cautious not to attract German mortar and artillery fire. To move above ground level was to risk being illuminated by flares and subjected to machinegun fire. In daylight snipers added to the hazards.

When the time came for VI Corps to break out, the western beachhead was seen by the Allies as being the place where a suitable distraction could be mounted. With the main thrust being planned towards Valmontone to cut the German lines of communication, a feint towards Rome would hold down enemy troops on the western flank and hinder their use in combating the Allied drive elsewhere.

1st and 5th British Divisions launched attacks which may have been seen as side-shows to those sitting in headquarters, but which were life-or-death matters to those who carried them out in the western beachhead. Amongst the actions that were fought that caused casualties to the units concerned were the Green Howards' raid and the Duke of Wellington's Regiment's attack on King's Arms and Green Bush Hill, which were mentioned in the overview chapter. The 2nd Battalion, The Royal Inniskilling Fusiliers, which since its arrival in Anzio in March had spent much of its time in the Lobster Claw and Fortress, was tasked with mounting an attack from the latter position on 29 May. Flanked by the 2nd Battalions of the Cameronians and the Wiltshires, the Inniskillings advanced through No-Man's-Land guided by two German deserters and under cover of an artillery bombardment. The deserters took them safely through the minefields and wire, into the enemy positions which were found to be empty – the Germans had withdrawn. Nothing was left but the detritus of war. For several miles the Inniskillings advanced through the wadi country behind German lines and across the Moletta River.

At dusk on the following day the battalion encountered the first signs of enemy resistance in front of Ardea, which it bypassed after night had fallen. Facing it now was its objective, the Banditella plateau, which overlooked the Via Laurentina, one of the roads to Rome, now less than twenty miles away. The plateau was taken with relatively little difficulty, only one of the three companies involved encountering enemy resistance, which was soon quashed. But the battalion was now exposed, the small plain which they had crossed by night en route to Banditella being overlooked by German positions from which artillery and machinegun fire was brought to bear on any attempt to bring forward supplies. Furthermore, the battalion positions on the plateau also came under fire, causing several casualties. The Inniskillings had bumped up against the Ardea Line, which extended from the Caesar Line and was the defence positions in front of Rome.

By 3 June the leading battalions of the 5th British Infantry Division had drawn level with the 'Skins. The Wiltshires attacked the enemy on the far side of the Via Laurentina, succeeding in taking their objective but at some cost. During the fight, Serjeant Maurice Rogers, already a holder of the Military Medal, earned the Victoria Cross for his action in pushing single-handedly into the enemy's defences, and act which threw them into confusion. Inspired by his leadership his platoon followed into the assault, while Serjeant Rogers, although wounded in the leg by a grenade, rushed a machinegun post in an attempt to silence it. He was killed at point-blank range, and

German prisoners taken at Anzio.

is buried in the Anzio Beachhead War Cemetery.

The Cameronians and the Inniskillings took up the attack as night fell, sending strong raiding parties to take key enemy positions. At dawn on 4 June the 'Skins prepared to launch a battalion attack; but the Germans had gone. Armoured cars from the 5th Reconnaisance Regiment passed through their lines and on up the Via Laurentina. A few hours later the battalion embussed on a fleet of trucks and followed; by nightfall they were on the River Tiber, five or six miles outside Rome, which the Americans had entered earlier. On 5 June some of the Inniskillings found their way into the Eternal City.

Chapter Four

CISTERNA

The actions covered in this chapter lie to the south of Cisterna. The small town of Isola Bella lies on the Cisterna-Borgo Montello road and there one may find a memorial to the fighting. Today much of the surrounding countryside is covered by fruit plantations, which effectively conceal the ground and make it difficult to imagine how it was in 1944. From the memorial the road leading north to Cisterna runs firstly across and then to the east of the ditch up which the leading Ranger companies moved when trying to take the town. Just before the railway bridge which crosses this road is a turning to the west. It was in drainage ditches along the southern side of this road, which leads to Carano and then Aprilia, that most of the companies fought out their battle.

The town of Cisterna was the objective of 3rd (US) Division during VI Corps' attempt to enlarge the beachhead at the end of January 1944. While 1st (British) Division was to advance up the Via Anziate to Campoleone, General Truscott's division was to push out through Cisterna and to go on to cut Highway 7. If matters progressed favourably, it would press on further to Velletri and even to Valmontone, to block Highway 6. The attack was originally scheduled to take place on 29 January, but it was postponed for twenty-four hours to allow the British and the newly-arrived Combat Command A to prepare for their part in the breakout operation. Unfortunately the delay also gave the Germans time to assemble their forces for the operation they were preparing to drive the Allies into the sea. Such are the fortunes of war.

For this operation, in addition to his own 3rd Division, General Truscott had the three battalions of Colonel Darby's Rangers and also Colonel Tucker's 504 Parachute Infantry Regiment under command. Facing this force he believed that the enemy consisted only of elements of the *Hermann Göring Panzer Division*, which intelligence believed to be thinly spread across the front and to include numbers of conscripted personnel from Poland and other eastern-European countries in its ranks, who were not expected to put up a strong resistance. To take advantage of these weaknesses, the VI Corps' plan for this sector was to attack in three places.

In the centre, 1st and 3rd Ranger Battalions were to infiltrate the German outposts under cover of darkness and seize Cisterna, which they would then hold and create havoc behind German lines. This would open the way for 15 Infantry Regiment and the 4th Ranger Battalion, who would advance an hour after the first offensive and join them in Cisterna. On the Allied right flank 504 Parachute Infantry Regiment would make a diversionary assault across the eastern fork of the Mussolini Canal, while on the left flank 7 Infantry Regiment would advance to Highway 7 and then to Cori, to the northwest of Cisterna. The attacks would be supported by armour and the divisional artillery.

Led by the 1st Battalion, the Rangers crossed the start line, a road running parallel to and about three and a half miles south of Highway 7, at 0100 hours on 30 January. The two Ranger

German soldiers from the *Hermann Göring Panzer Division* on the Anzio front.

Isola Bella and Cisterna (in the distance). The drainage ditch up which the Rangers advanced can be seen to the right of the crossroads, before passing beneath the road and dividing.

battalions then moved towards Cisterna in single file along the Pantano Ditch which ran between known enemy positions to a point about one and a half miles south of the town. Thereafter they would have to advance over open ground. Apart from the ditches and isolated farmhouses, there was no cover.

Colonel William O Darby controlled the operation from a farmhouse off the Cisterna to Isola Bella road. The first indication he had that things were not progressing smoothly was when four radio operators who should have been with the advancing troops reported that they were lost. Communications with his battalions would not be as well-catered for as he had hoped. Next, the 1st and 3rd Battalions became separated. The 1st Battalion Commander, Major Jack Dobson, continued to advance with three companies while the remaining three halted to await the other battalion. Captain Shunstrom took command of the rearmost companies and dispatched a runner to find the 3rd Battalion, which should have been close on his heels. When contact was established

Colonel William O Darby.

with this unit, he was told that its commander had been killed by a German tank shell. The Germans were obviously aware that there was movement in the area, but they did not mount a systematic operation to stop the Rangers; indeed, the advancing Americans were unhindered and succeeded in removing two groups of enemy sentries silently, with knives.

At about 0545 hours, as night began to turn into day, the first three companies of Rangers attempted to rush Cisterna, hoping to cross the open ground in front of them before dawn broke. Some 600 yards south of the town they ran into a German encampment, where they surprised the enemy and dispatched a number of them with knives and bayonets. Another 400 yards on, they were halted by heavy fire from the town, from farmhouses, foxholes and ditches, and the leading group of Rangers was forced to take cover in a drainage ditch.

The second group of Rangers, the three companies from 1st Battalion and the 3rd Battalion, got to within 300 yards of the leading group, when they also ran into Germans. Shunstrom managed to get through to his battalion commander with three men; as he was being briefed, three German tanks appeared behind the 3rd Battalion – the Rangers were cut off. Despite disabling these tanks with bazooka fire, the ring was closing. The 3rd Battalion group was strung out along the ditch up which they had advanced, which was not the place to fight from.

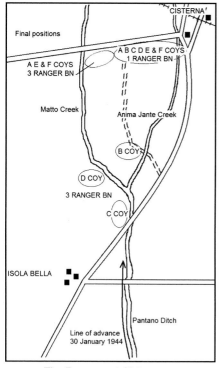

The Rangers at Cisterna.

The Germans succeeded in driving the Americans into a perimeter about 300 yards in diameter. With no cover but drainage ditches, and with no weapons or ammunition other than that which they had carried with them, time was beginning to run out. Attempts to break out were fruitless. As the ammunition stocks began to disappear, the men of three companies which had been gathered as a reserve in the centre of the

178

perimeter passed half of their ammunition to those manning the front line.

The battle grew ever more desperate as the German noose closed. Major Dobson was wounded while destroying a Mark IV tank: he had shot the commander with his pistol before climbing aboard it to toss a phosphorous grenade into the open hatch, and been hit when leaping back to the ground. Both battalions were now without their commanders. Blocking the escape route back to American lines were some seventeen German tanks and self-propelled guns, which proceeded to overrun the Rangers' positions, but not without considerable loss to themselves - only two remained intact, the remainder being taken out by bazookas, sticky bombs and grenades. Two tank crews were dispatched by a group of Rangers who commandeered their tanks and attempted to drive them through the German lines, only to have them destroyed by other Rangers who could not have known who was in them. Regardless of these efforts, the German stranglehold held firm. Two companies of the 3rd Battalion were able to move closer towards Cisterna and the 1st Battalion positions, but with their ammunition steadily depleting there was little point; it was becoming only a matter of time before they lost the battle.

Attacks by tanks and infantry apart, the small perimeter was pounded by enemy artillery and Nebelwerfer fire. Multi-barrelled antiaircraft guns added to the weight of shells thrown against the Rangers, crouching in their ditches with no heavy weapons available to fight back. With inadequate com-munications to the rear, they were unable to adjust fire from their own artillery to relieve the pressure upon them.

German tanks were brought up to fire down the length of the ditch in which the 3rd Battalion survivors were trapped, creating heavy casualties. Many of the wounded were bayoneted by the Germans; some Rangers were taken prisoner and pushed into a group surrounded by German paratroops supported by two tanks and an armoured car, before being marched towards the 1st Battalion positions. Dobson and his men opened fire when the group was 300 yards away, killing some of the enemy; in response the Germans shot and bayoneted some of their prisoners, then pushed the rest in front of them as they continued to advance. An English-speaking officer demanded the surrender of Dobson's men, an order backed up by the killing of more prisoners to underline the gravity of the situation. With nothing left with which to continue the fight but their knives and bare hands, there was little alternative but to surrender. Small groups of Rangers attempted to escape, but almost all were killed or taken prisoner in the attempt – of the 767 men who had set out early that morning, only six made it back to Allied lines. Among those killed was the medical officer of the 3rd Battalion, who had objected to his German guards separating him from the wounded men under his care. He took a pistol from one of the enemy and shot him, only to be shot in his turn by a second German.

The two Ranger battalions were not the only ones to suffer heavily: only one man escaped from the forty-three strong platoon of the 3rd Reconnaissance Troop which was supporting the Rangers.

As the 1st and 3rd Battalions were undergoing their ordeal by fire, the 4th Battalion had been fighting its way forward, having crossed the start line an hour after the others. After about half a mile it ran into unexpected enemy resistance, coming under machinegun fire from both sides of the road. Two machinegun nests were overrun at the point of the bayonet, but there were more which could not be fought through. To add to the Rangers' problems, German artillery fire began to descend on the area. With fifty per cent casualties, it could do nothing to assist the other battalions – who themselves suffered a ninety-nine percent casualty rate. 15 Infantry Regiment, which followed the 4th Battalion, was not able to take Isola Bella until the afternoon. Tanks and tank destroyers had to drive German defenders from the village ruins.

On the eastern flank, 504 Parachute Infantry ran into the *7th Luftwaffe Jäger Battalion* and heavy artillery fire and were unable to make ground. A stalemate began which was to last for eight weeks, and trench warfare became the order of the day.

To the west, the 1st Battalion of 7 Infantry Regiment was trapped in the open by flares and automatic weapon fire from two hillocks as it advanced during the early hours of the morning. It suffered nearly 150 casualties before it was able to extricate itself.

German propaganda understandably made the most of the situation. The Ranger prisoners were paraded through Rome,

BATTAGLIA DI
CISTERNA ANZIO APRILIA
LOCALITA' ISOLABELLA
FEMMINA MORTA
ON THIS SITE
THOUSANDS OF MEN
FOUGT AND DIED

AN DIESEM ORT
TAUSEND VON MENSCHEN
KAMPFTE UND FIELEN

IN QUESTO LUOGO
MIGLIAIA DI UOMINI
COMBATTERONO E MORIRONO

1944 1994

while Axis Sally gloated that 'the Rangers have at last entered Rome, but they have come not as conquerors but as our prisoners'. Several of them took the opportunity to escape from their captors while they were in the Eternal City.

The Ranger force was no longer a viable formation; within weeks it was disbanded, and the survivors were returned to the United States

The memorial at Isola Bella.

or absorbed into the First Special Service Force.

From the German perspective, an Allied advance at Cisterna was not unexpected. As with the Via Anziate to the west, the road network in or out of the beachhead offered only limited choices, and – given the nature of the off-road ground – there was no real option for the Allies or the Germans but to keep to what roads there were. The tank-trap nature of the ditch-scored countryside on the eastern side of the beachhead severely limited movement. With the objective of driving the Allies into the sea, Kesselring's men were bound to assemble at Cisterna, just as they did at Campoleone. The Rangers walked directly into a strong German force preparing to move across the same ground, but in the opposite direction; had General Lucas stuck to his original timetable for the attack – 29 January – the enemy would have had a day's less time to gather, and it is possible that the fortunes would have been reversed.

By the day of the attack, the German forces gathered near Cisterna included all of the *Hermann Göring Panzer Division,* elements of *26th Panzer Division,* a regiment of paratroops and the Machinegun Battalion of the *4th Parachute Regiment.* A Pole serving in the German army had deserted and had tried to warn the Americans of the increased enemy numbers in the area; he was evacuated to the rear and his story did not emerge until he was routinely interrogated at Fifth Army Headquarters. By then, the battle was over.

The decision to delay the 3rd Division attack had given the Germans time to assemble sufficient troops to repel it. By a twist of fate the attack, unsuccessful that it may have been, forced Germans to delay their offensive against the beachhead until 4 February, which in turn gave VI Corps more time to prepare for it.

Chapter Five

THE EASTERN BEACHHEAD

The beachhead was bordered to the east by the Mussolini Canal, in places 170 feet wide and twelve to twenty feet deep, and for much of its length having an embankment on both sides. Dug to drain the Pontine Marshes, the ditch formed a very effective antitank barrier and was a naturally strong line on which to form the initial perimeter. Today renamed the Canale di Moscarello, it still gives a good impression of its condition in 1944 – and it still makes a formidable obstacle. Running into the canal are smaller channels, forming a latticework of ditches which provide much of the cover in the area. The countryside between the drainage ditches is flat and featureless, and was to become known as the 'Billiard Table' by the men who fought here. Now with avenues of trees along the roads, at the time of the battle the ground was largely clear of any but the lowest vegetation, and there was little to provide concealment from view.

Immediately after the landing on 22 January the line was occupied by 3rd (US) Division, and during the attempted breakout from the beachhead at the end of January 504 Parachute Infantry had attacked eastwards from here to provide a diversion from the main 3rd Division advance towards Cisterna. 179 Infantry Regiment then took over the line for a short while until the unit was replaced by the First Special Service Force, which arrived in the beachhead on 2 February.

The First Special Service Force had been formed in 1942 by Lieutenant Colonel (to be Brigadier General by the time of Anzio) Robert T Frederick. It was intended that the Force would be employed on the most difficult missions, the first of which was to be a diversionary attack deep behind enemy lines in Norway. This particular operation never took place, but by the time it was cancelled the unit had been raised and trained in parachuting, skiing, demolitions and in the use of a wide range of weapons. It was made up of three two-battalion regiments (rather than the three battalions that comprised the standard

183

Brigadier General Robert T Frederick.

American Army regiment). It was too valuable an asset to be disbanded.

A 2,500-strong elite force, it was manned by both Canadian and American soldiers. While the Canadians represented some of the best of that nation's soldiers, the initial response from some American commanders when asked to nominate men for the new formation was to off-load the troublemakers from their units. It must be recorded, however, that the unit also attracted numbers of American volunteers looking for a challenge – much as had happened with the British airborne and commando forces. Canadians and Americans served without segregation or discrimination in the same platoons and companies, and all were uniformed and equipped by the US Army. The only source of friction between the two nationalities appears to have been in the discrepancies in rates of pay, which were higher for those coming from south of the border. It is understandable, but perhaps regrettable, that these men who fought together were separated in death, for the Americans who died here while serving with the Force are buried in the Nettuno Cemetery while the Canadians rest in the Commonwealth War Graves Commission graveyards.

First Special Service Force arrived in Italy two months after the Salerno landings. Here it was attached to the 36th (US) Division and spearheaded Fifth Army's advance on Monte la Difensa and Monte la Remetanea, which guarded the entrance to the Mignano Gap, southeast of Cassino. Frederick's troops scaled the heights at night and caught the Germans unprepared, but lost nearly a third of their strength in the fighting that followed.

When it arrived in the Anzio beachhead on 2 February the First Special Service Force numbered sixty-eight officers and 1,165 men, which allowed it an average of one man for each eleven yards on the eight mile front that it held along the Mussolini Canal. From the sea inland, the canal was crossed by a number of bridges, numbered from the coast and progressing

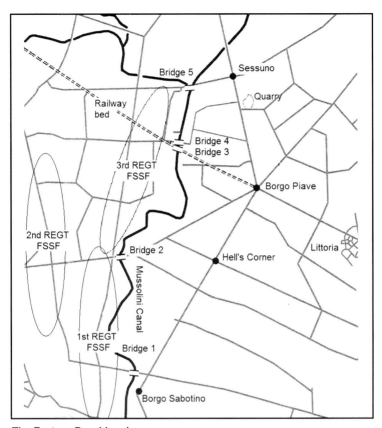

The Eastern Beachhead.

inland. The 3rd Regiment held the line from Bridge 5 downstream to Bridge 2, and 1st Regiment the remaining length, to where the canal entered the sea. 2nd Regiment, with its two battalions now merged into one because of the casualty figures, was held in reserve behind the line.

Partly to defend the length of front with the limited manpower, but also to assert themselves and to intimidate the enemy, the Force adopted an aggressive role from the outset, mounting reconnaissance patrols and raids in numbers of up to battalion strength. The intention was to take control of the area and to dominate the Germans. Particularly during the hours of darkness, the Forcemen were active in penetrating the German lines to take prisoners, kill the enemy, and to destroy houses and other positions which the enemy might be using as observation posts or for shelter. A well-practiced technique was to distract the attention of Germans occupying a house by firing a bazooka shell into it while explosives were placed to blow up the building – and its inhabitants. A major part of the work was to locate artillery emplacements, which could then be brought under counter-battery fire.

In the face of such assertive action during the first week of the Force arriving, the Germans withdrew their front line some half-mile, leaving a no-man's land between them and the Allies. Control of this gap became an ongoing struggle, in which the Germans took possession of the isolated farmhouses and small villages during the day, while the Forcemen infiltrated to eject them by night. With blackened faces, it was not long before the Germans came to believe, firstly, that they were facing coloured troops. The Force soon became known as the 'Black Devils' to the *Hermann Göring Panzer Division* which faced it across the canal.

The Force's projection across the front line did not stop with reconnaissance and raiding expeditions. Borgo Sabotino, the village closest to the coast and on the eastern side of the canal,

The lunar appearance of the Mussolini Canal bank, caused by American dugouts.

about a quarter of a mile behind German lines, was occupied by the Forcemen after driving the enemy out. Renamed 'Gusville' after First Lieutenant Gus Heilman, one of their officers, the Forcemen elected to stay. With Heilman as self-appointed mayor, the village soon had a bar and a chief of police appointed from the members of his platoon. Fresh meat, eggs and vegetables were obtained by raiding deep behind German positions and from gardening, and wine was 'liberated' from the cellars of Nettuno. Gardening became an obsession for some men, who pursued their interest during daylight hours and patrolled at night. The village chapel was the site for weekly church services. All of this activity, of course, did not go unremarked by the Germans: the main road through the village was named 'Tank Street' because of the tank shells which regularly flew along it.

The fame of Gusville was also widespread through the Allied ranks, where it was a potent morale booster for troops suffering their enforced and cramped stay in the beachhead. The ability of the Forcemen to regard their situation as one that could be improved upon and made the best of, rather than considering themselves as being in a seriously tight corner, was both refreshing and liberating. Gusville also attracted the attention of the press, who began writing about it in the *Stars and Stripes*. In response, the troops in Gusville produced their own version of the *Herald Tribune*, and the Force itself began its own newssheet, *The Braves Bulletin* ('Braves' being the name by which the Force was known when it was first raised).

If the activities of the Force raised Allied morale, they had the opposite effect on the enemy. The ceaseless patrolling and raids, together with the silent killing of sentries and outposts (all Forcemen were trained in unarmed combat and issued with knives) began to wear on German nerves. A particularly effective Force technique with which to pile on the psychological pressure was to leave cards displaying the unit insignia and the words 'Das dicke ende kommt noch!' ('The worst is yet to come') on the bodies of enemy dead. Word spread in the enemy ranks that the Forcemen took no prisoners, and while there were doubtless occasions when they did not, this was far from being a hard and fast rule - on one February night alone they bagged 111 Germans in a trap laid near Borgo Sabotino.

First Special Service Force raid on the Eastern Beachhead.

The enemy units that the Force faced on the far side of the canal were firstly the *Hermann Göring Panzer Division*, which included parachute, panzer, panzer grenadier and flak units. Other enemy units encountered included elements of *7th zbV*, a *Luftwaffe* penal battalion, and *16* and *36 SS Regiments*. There were also Italian Fascist units: the *Italian SS Infantry*, the *Militia Armata*, the *Barbarigo Battalion* and the *San Marco Marines*.

One area which was raided on several occasions was known as the Quarry, which lay to the east of the Sessuno (now Borgo Podgora) – Borgo Piave road. Heavily defended by the Germans, it sheltered artillery pieces which fired deep into American positions; south of Borgo Piave on the road to Borgo Sabotino is a crossroads known to the Forcemen as Hell's Corner. Placid today, and set among avenues of eucalyptus trees, the crossroads gives no indication of the carnage that was wrought there in 1944, when the ground was littered with bodies which neither side could readily remove. The Germans laced the area liberally with mines, which the Forcemen had little option but to walk through without benefit of detectors because of the time and noise that clearing operations would have involved. On one large-scale night raid the Force strayed into a field strewn with schu- and anti-tank mines; they sustained thirty-two casualties with legs or feet lost. In the three months that the Special Service Force was on the Mussolini Canal line eighty-nine men were killed, captured, or were listed as missing in action.

In preparation for the breakout, the Force was replaced on the canal by 36 (US) Engineer Combat Regiment on 9 May 1944. The Force was to work with 3rd (US) Division in its part in Operation BUFFALO.

INDEX